D0379497

Other books by Lois Lowry:

The One Hundredth Thing About Caroline

Switcharound

Anastasia Krupnik

Anastasia Again!

Autumn Street

The Silent Boy

All rights reserved. Originally published in hardcover in the United States
by Houghton Mifflin Books for Children, an imprint of
Houghton Mifflin Harcourt, 1990.

For information about permission to reproduce selections from this book,
write to trade.permissions@hmhco.com or to Permissions, Houghton
Mifflin Harcourt Publishing Company, 3 Park Avenue, 19th Floor,
New York, New York 10016.

www.hmhco.com

Book design by Rebecca Bond and Monica Liaw.
The text of this book is set in Adobe Garamond Pro.

The Library of Congress has cataloged the hardcover edition as follows:
Lowry, Lois.
Your move, J.P.! / Lois Lowry.
p. cm.
Summary: Lovestruck J.P. finds himself doing all sorts of weird things
to impress his new interest but his life becomes very complicated when a
simple lie gets out of control.
[1. Interpersonal relations — Fiction. 2. Honesty — Fiction.
3. Schools — Fiction] I. Title.
PZ7.L9673Yo 1990   89-24707
[Fic] — dc20   CIP AC

ISBN: 978-0-395-53639-1 hardcover
ISBN: 978-1-328-75067-9 paperback

Manufactured in the United States of America
DOC 10 9 8 7 6 5 4 3 2 1
4500695181

Just the Tates!

Book 3

Your Move, J.P.!

by LOIS LOWRY

HOUGHTON MIFFLIN HARCOURT

BOSTON NEW YORK

ONE

It was an April morning—a Tuesday morning, to be exact—a morning that had nothing whatsoever unusual about it. The sun was shining, the trash had been collected from the sidewalk, the breakfast toast was moderately burned but still edible, and the various clocks in the apartment, which never agreed exactly, indicated that it was somewhere close to seven-thirty a.m.

It was a morning just exactly like every other Tuesday morning in April on the West Side of New York City, except for one thing.

James Priestly Tate, age twelve, had an overwhelming urge, for the first time in his life, to use deodorant.

He tried to ignore it at first. But he found that he was not able to put on his shirt. His arms were paralyzed. When he attempted to manipulate his arms to enter the armholes of the light blue button-down shirt that was part of the uniform he wore every day to school, they wouldn't move. They weren't ready to move toward those armholes—and they wouldn't be ready until James Priestly Tate used deodorant.

Frowning, J.P. headed back to the bathroom of the apartment. He had already been there once, and brushed his teeth. J.P. was a dedicated, almost religious toothbrusher. He had been devoted to brushing his teeth from the time he was three years old and a dentist uncle had given him a green toothbrush with a frog's face on the handle.

He had already combed his hair and tied his shoes. He was wearing his chino pants, also part of his school uniform.

But he was shirtless when he stood at the

bathroom door, thumped on it with his fist, and called to his ten-year-old sister inside.

"Caroline, hurry up!"

"I can't hurry up, I'm in the shower! You had your turn already. I thought you were all through with the bathroom!"

"I forgot something. I need something," J.P. called through the closed door.

"What do you need?" Caroline called back. "I'll hand it out."

Oh, great. J.P. couldn't stand his sister to begin with, and now he had to call his most intimate needs to her through a bathroom door. He should forget the whole thing. But he couldn't. He had this overwhelming urge to use deodorant. He couldn't figure it out. He didn't even *smell*. It wasn't as if he had just run the marathon or something. But he had this urge; and the urge was so great that he was even willing to embarrass himself in front of Caroline.

"Deodorant!" he bellowed through the door.

He heard the sound of the shower stop. He heard the rustle of the shower curtain. He heard the door of the medicine cabinet click open. Then the bath-room door opened an inch, and his sister's hand appeared. It thrust a plastic container at him.

"Here," Caroline said, and closed the door again.

J.P. looked down at the pale green aerosol can, which was decorated with yellow flowers. He uncapped it and sniffed it. He looked at its name: Sunny Meadow.

He made a face. He wanted deodorant. He maybe even needed deodorant. Certainly he had an overwhelming urge to use deodorant.

But he didn't want to enter his seventh-grade homeroom smelling like a sunny meadow.

He headed for the kitchen, where his mother was cleaning up the breakfast dishes.

"Hi," Joanna Tate said cheerfully. "Where's your shirt?"

J.P. didn't answer. He held out the bottle of Sunny Meadow toward her. "Is there any other deodorant in this apartment?" he asked.

She shook her head. "No. Why?"

"This is too feminine," J.P. explained. "It smells like flowers."

"Well, of course it does. That's why I like it. Also, it's cheaper than some of the others."

"Next time you go shopping, would you buy something with a more masculine smell, and something with a more masculine *name?*"

Mrs. Tate nodded. "I guess so. I didn't know you even used deodorant, James. You smell okay to me." Then she stared at him affectionately for a moment. "But I forget how old you're getting. Twelve. My goodness. You're an adolescent already. Next thing I know, you'll start *shaving.* Let me see your chin for a minute."

She reached for J.P.'s chin, cupped her hand around it, and held it up toward the light. He pulled away, irritated.

"My chin's *fine,*" he muttered. "I don't need to shave. I just want to deal with my pits, is all. But I don't want to smell like wildflowers."

"What would you like to smell like?" his mother asked, turning back to the breakfast table. "Locker room? Auto body repair shop?"

"Ha ha," J.P. muttered, heading back to his room. His sister, Caroline, appeared in the hall, combing her damp hair, wearing her bathrobe. "Jockstrap?" she suggested cheerfully. "Super Bowl?"

"Quit eavesdropping," J.P. said. He entered his bedroom and picked up the blue shirt that he had left on his unmade bed. He dropped the Sunny Meadow deodorant unopened on his desk and finished dressing. Tomorrow, he thought. Tomorrow he would use deodorant, and tomorrow maybe he would smell strong and masculine and pleasant during second period when he went to math class and sat down in his seat next to—

J.P. blushed, all alone in his room, with his shirt half-buttoned. *That* was it, he realized. Be honest with yourself, Tate; it's because there was that empty seat next to yours in math class, and now all of a sudden it isn't empty anymore because that new student arrived last week and was assigned that seat, and now instead of an empty seat beside you in math class there is an *occupied* seat, and it is occupied by—

He blushed again. Say it, Tate, he told himself. Say the name. Say it *aloud*.

J.P. took a deep breath. He checked to be certain

that the door to his bedroom was tightly closed, so that his eavesdropping sister wouldn't overhear. And he said it.

"Angela Patricia Galsworthy," he said reverently. He could almost hear violins playing in the background as he said the name aloud.

He could hardly believe it. It had never occurred to him, in his twelve—almost thirteen—years of life, that this might someday happen. Now it had.

James Priestly Tate was in love.

The Burke-Thaxter School was a very small private school. Everyone knew everyone else. The kindergarten kids knew the high school kids. All the students knew the gray-haired janitor, Mr. Donovan, as well as they knew their own grandparents. The entire fifth grade had been invited to the wedding when their teacher, Ms. Jackson, got married; she had sent each one of them—there were thirteen fifth-graders—a postcard from her honeymoon in Acapulco. And now that she was married and her new name was Ms. Jackson-Wyden, all the students, even those in the other grades, watched her husband,

Stan Wyden, when he did his nightly newscast on television, even if they weren't at all interested in the news.

When a new student enrolled in the school, everyone knew about it. So it was not surprising that Angela Galsworthy was well known: not only in the seventh grade but throughout the Burke-Thaxter School.

Unlike most new kids, she hadn't entered at the beginning of the school year. She had arrived and been introduced to the class on a Monday morning in mid-April, just last week.

"Class," said Mr. Goldfine, J.P.'s homeroom teacher, "I'd like you to meet, ah" — he looked at the card in his hand — "Angela Patricia Galsworthy, who has moved here from, ah" — he looked again — "my goodness, London."

J.P. had looked up from the *Smithsonian* magazine he'd been reading at his desk. J.P. was not at all interested in girls, and it was somewhat surprising that he looked up at all. But Mr. Goldfine had a loud voice, and the article J.P. was reading wasn't very interesting. So he looked up. And when he did, he blinked.

Angela Patricia Galsworthy was wearing the Burke-Thaxter uniform, so her clothes weren't at all interesting. They were the same clothes that all the girls, including J.P.'s sister, Caroline, wore every day to school.

But her hair! Her hair was long and blond, freshly washed, and it looked like—*spun gold,* thought J.P.

And her teeth! She was smiling at the class, and she didn't have braces like so many of the girls, and her teeth were straight and white, and they looked like—*pearls,* thought J.P.

Her eyes! They were a deep blue-green, large and fringed with long lashes, and they looked like—*pools,* thought J.P.

Her skin! It was the same shade as a pale, translucent dish that his mother had inherited from a great-aunt and kept high on a shelf so that it wouldn't break. Her skin was like—*porcelain,* J.P. thought, remembering the word that described the dish.

Then he blushed, cringed, and slouched in his

seat, lifting the magazine again. He couldn't believe the thoughts he'd been having. Hair like spun gold; teeth like pearls; eyes like pools; skin like porcelain. Cool it, J.P., he said to himself. For a moment there you were writing a trashy novel. You're *sick*.

He could see, suddenly, that the girl was about to speak. J.P. tried to impose deafness on himself because he didn't want to listen. For the first time he envied Kevin Kerrigan, his classmate who wore a hearing aid. Kevin could just switch his aid off whenever he wanted to.

Turn off, J.P. commanded his ears. It is not in your best interest to listen to this.

But for the first time, J.P.'s phenomenal will-power didn't work, and he heard Angela Patricia Galsworthy greet the seventh grade.

"Good morning," he heard her say. "I'm terribly pleased to meet all of you."

And her voice! Her voice was like — oh, *no,* J.P. told himself; don't even think it — but he did. Her voice, he thought, against his will, was like a *rippling brook*.

He didn't look up. His face felt flushed and

warm. His stomach lurched. His hands itched. His shoes seemed suddenly to be too small; his toes hurt. Quickly J.P. flipped the pages of *Smithsonian* and began to read much more than he had ever wanted to know about alligators.

He had known the terrible truth that morning, though he hadn't admitted it, even to himself. Now—just a few days later—he realized that it was something he had to face. He would face it with courage and a stiff upper lip and valor and—J.P. winced—yes, he would face it with deodorant.

Slowly he unbuttoned his shirt and, with his eyes closed because that seemed to make it easier, he sprayed himself with Sunny Meadow.

He knew he was doomed.

Two

J.P. GLANCED THROUGH THE WINDOW of his English classroom while Mrs. Hunt talked endlessly about the book they were reading, *The Prince and the Pauper*. He had read the assigned chapters—J.P. always did his homework—but he thought the book was one of the most boring he'd ever encountered. Even Mrs. Hunt, whom he liked, couldn't seem to make it interesting.

He felt a tap on his shoulder, and Hope Delafield passed him a folded piece of paper. J.P. unfolded it and read: B-B5ch. He thought for a moment and then grinned. Good old Hopie. She had him in check. He and Hope had been playing a chess game on paper for two weeks now and it was at a crucial point. J.P. was the chess champion of the whole school, but Hope, the only girl in the chess club, was a pretty good competitor and getting better all the time.

J.P. would have to come up with a supergenius maneuver to get his king out of check. He tried to envision the chess board in his mind. Ordinarily he had no trouble doing that. Ordinarily he could see his next move almost instantly. But today the chess game seemed almost as boring as *The Prince and the Pauper*. J.P. stared at the paper, and then his eyes drifted to the window again.

Outside, a misty breeze was moving the branches on a scrawny tree, and across the street two pigeons were fighting on the window ledge of an apartment building.

J.P. had never paid attention to pigeons before. New York City, especially this area near Central Park, was filled with pigeons, so many that he didn't notice them unless they flew low directly above him and he had to worry about the possibility of them depositing something disgusting on his head. But now he watched these two peck and flutter, and he wondered if maybe they were male pigeons fighting over a female. On a nearby ledge, a pale gray pigeon sat quietly and observed the quarrel.

That's the female, J.P. decided. To me she looks just like any dumb pigeon. But to *those* guys—he glanced again at the warring pair—she probably has the prettiest face, the softest coo, the sleekest wingspan. They probably feel as if they can't live without her.

His gaze shifted to the back of Angela Galsworthy's blond head. Today her hair was tied back in a ponytail, and he could see her right earlobe quite clearly. It looked like a tiny seashell, pale pink and perfectly curved.

Carefully, with his ballpoint pen, J.P. drew Angela Galsworthy's earlobe on the lined sheet of loose-leaf paper that lay on his desktop waiting for a chess move.

"*Weird,* Tate." J.P. heard a whisper, and he saw Kevin Kerrigan, the nosiest person in the seventh grade, leaning over from his desk, peering at the paper.

J.P. scowled at Kevin and covered the paper with his hand. It *was* weird, he thought. Earlobe to rook 1? Embarrassed, he scribbled over the earlobe and tried to concentrate on the chess move.

Mrs. Hunt's voice droned on. "So you see," she was saying, "the prince, wearing the pauper's clothes, finds himself on London Bridge. Has anyone here ever visited London?"

A few hands shot up. Not J.P.'s. He'd hardly ever been outside New York City, except for the few times when he had visited his father in Des Moines.

"Oh, Angela, of course!" Mrs. Hunt exclaimed, and J.P. jumped at the sound of the name. He looked over, beyond the earlobe, and saw Angela Galsworthy's slender left arm — it had some pale golden hairs on it, he noticed, and a delicate silver watch on its wrist — in the air.

"I almost forgot, Angela," Mrs. Hunt went on, "but of course London is your home, isn't it?"

Angela Galsworthy nodded shyly.

"Did you by any chance live near London Bridge?" Mrs. Hunt asked.

"Oh, no," Angela said. "London Bridge is down near the Tower of London. My house is on Old Church Crescent, not far from Battersea Bridge. The river curves about quite a bit, you see—oh, goodness, it's terribly difficult to explain. It would be easier to explain if I had a map."

J.P. watched her as she talked. He felt warm all over—probably his deodorant was failing him, he was so warm—listening to her waterfall voice, with its British accent.

"Do you have a map of London at home, by any chance?" Mrs. Hunt asked.

"No, I'm sorry," Angela said, shaking her head.

"I'm afraid I don't, either. Class, does anyone happen to have a map of London at home? Someone who could get together with Angela to sort out the geography of this book?"

So many hands shot into the air, it looked as if a foul ball had gone into the stands at a Yankees game. J.P. looked around. Nicholas Kostas had his hand up. Danny Calhoun. Antonio Valdez. Kevin

Kerrigan was waving his as if he were trying to hail a taxi.

All boys. That's odd, J.P. thought. No girls have maps of London at home. But practically every boy in seventh-grade English does.

Mrs. Hunt was laughing. "Amazing," she said. "Well, let's see. J.P., how about you? Would you get your map tonight, and then in the morning you and Angela can go over it, before English class?"

J.P. put his hand down. He looked at his arm in amazement. It had taken on a life of its own, completely independent of his brain. He hadn't even known that it had been in the air. "Sure," he said to Mrs. Hunt.

Angela looked over at him and smiled.

J.P. bent his head and stared at the paper on his desk. Hastily he wrote in a chess move, K-R1, folded the paper, leaned across the aisle, and handed it back to Hope Delafield.

The class ended. The students gathered their books and moved in a group toward the door. Angela Galsworthy, surrounded by a cluster of giggling girls, headed toward her next class. Danny

Calhoun shoved Nicholas Kostas against the wall. "You jerk," he muttered. "You don't know London from Hoboken, New Jersey."

Kevin Kerrigan punched his best friend, Antonio Valdez, in the arm. Antonio rubbed the punched place, and both boys turned to glare at J.P. "Big London expert, huh?" Kevin jeered. "I bet you don't even have a map of the New York subway!"

J.P. ignored them. He went to the pencil sharpener on the windowsill and began to sharpen a pencil nonchalantly.

From the doorway of the emptying room, Hope called to him in triumphant surprise. "Checkmate, J.P.!" she called, waving the piece of notebook paper. "No kidding! First time I've ever beaten you!"

J.P. blinked. He didn't even remember what chess move he had written down. He didn't even care.

The only thing he cared about was figuring out how to find a map of London before school tomorrow.

J.P. adjusted the backpack that held his schoolbooks and walked glumly to the corner, where he would get the crosstown bus home. He could see his sister, Caroline, in her school uniform, waiting there already, with two of her fifth-grade friends. She waved.

He ignored her and leaned over to poke in a trash container, hoping that by chance someone had thrown a map of London away. No luck. There were several newspapers, an empty wine bottle, and Nicholas Kostas's crumpled history exam, with a B– written in red ink across the top.

The bus appeared, hissing its brakes, and Caroline called, "Come on, J.P.!"

He ignored her again, pretending that she was a total stranger, and boarded the bus. As usual, no seats. J.P. stood wedged between two overweight people and thought about his problem as the bus moved across New York City, stopping jerkily from time to time.

A bookstore would be the solution. And there was a small bookstore just down the street from the Tates' apartment building. J.P. wiggled his left arm up past the hips of the beefy woman next to him and looked at his watch. Three forty-five. Okay. Great.

He could get to the bookstore before it closed, and he could invest in a map of London and his future with Angela Galsworthy.

J.P. relaxed. He took a deep breath, standing in his squashed position, and became aware that his height made him level with adult armpits. He wished that more people on the bus had used Sunny Meadow deodorant.

"Too expensive? Jeez, kid, it's only eight ninety-five. Whaddaya expect, that we *give* books away?"

The bookstore clerk peered over the counter at J.P., who held the paperback guide to London in his hand.

"Could I pay you two dollars now, maybe, and bring the rest in next week?" J.P. suggested politely.

The clerk didn't bother to answer.

"Well, do you have a Xerox machine? Could I just Xerox the map?"

The clerk began sorting through some credit card receipts.

J.P. shifted his weight from one foot to the other. He opened the book again to the map of London.

Maybe he could memorize it and then draw it from memory when he got home.

But he realized, looking at the map, that it would be impossible. London was too complicated, even for a phenomenal memory like J.P. Tate's. The streets of New York City made sense, numbered as they were. He could probably draw a New York City map from memory. But London was a haphazard maze of streets, with the river zigzagging through the middle, crisscrossed with bridges. And all the streets had weird names, unlike New York, with its solid, sensible Sixty-Ninth and Fifth and Forty-Second and Third. London had—J.P. squinted, looking at the tiny print—Chelsea Embankment, Marylebone Road, Montagu Square, Porchester Gardens, Cleveland Terrace, St. John's Wood Road. He closed the book slowly and looked once more at the clerk with what he hoped was a pleading, *needy* look. But the clerk had turned away and was dialing the telephone.

J.P. put the book on the counter, left the store, and headed home. He could picture Mrs. Hunt tomorrow, staring at him, saying in front of the class,

"But, J.P., you said that you had a map of London at home. Weren't you telling the truth?"

He could picture all the guys: Nicholas, Antonio, Kevin, and Danny. They would hoot with derisive laughter, he knew, making a fool of him in front of—

He groaned. He could picture Angela Galsworthy, looking at him in surprise, her pink moist mouth rounded into an open O. She wouldn't sneer and taunt him, he knew, not a soft-spoken, high-class person like Angela Patricia Galsworthy; but she would never care for him again. She would turn her back on him forever. He would become, for Angela Galsworthy, The Boy Who Had Lied.

Caroline was sitting on the front steps, her schoolbooks beside her, looking at baseball cards with little Billy DeVito, who lived on the first floor.

"Where did you go?" she asked. "You got off the bus when I did, but then you disappeared."

"Bookstore," J.P. said tersely.

"Oh." Caroline turned back to Billy, who had handed her a new card, and she examined Reggie Jackson admiringly.

"Caroline," J.P. said suddenly, "can you loan me seven dollars?"

She stared at him. "*Seven dollars?* What do you think I am, a bank? I don't have seven dollars."

J.P. sighed. "Is Mom home?" he asked.

"Of course not. It's only four-fifteen. She never gets home from work till five-thirty. Anyway, she wouldn't lend you seven dollars. She was complaining this morning that she can't afford to pay the whole phone bill this month. Remember, she said if we call Dad in Des Moines any more, we have to do it collect?"

J.P. remembered. "Yeah," he said gloomily.

"What do you need it for, anyway?" Caroline handed the pack of baseball cards back to Billy and looked up quizzically at her brother.

J.P. started up the steps. "I need to buy a map of London," he told his sister. Then he looked back at Billy DeVito, who was patiently sorting his baseball cards. "Billy, do you by any chance have a map of London?"

Billy looked up at him. "No," he said, cheerfully. "But I have two Oil Can Boyds."

Three

"It's because of that new girl, isn't it? Isn't it?" Caroline asked as she trudged up the stairs behind J.P. "Tell the truth. It's because of that girl from England. What's her name—Andrea?"

J.P. didn't say anything. He rummaged through his pocket for the key, opened the door, and entered the apartment. Caroline followed him, still talking. "Alexandra? Is that her name? Come on, J.P. *Talk*."

J.P. flung his backpack onto the couch and began pulling open the drawers to his mother's desk in the living room. He found a packet of maps and slipped off the rubber band that held them together.

New Jersey.

Pennsylvania.

Connecticut.

And a guide to New York museums. *Great.* Just great. He frowned and tossed them back into the drawer.

"Mom doesn't have a map of London," Caroline announced from the kitchen, where she was pouring herself a glass of milk. "You're wasting your time. You want some milk?"

J.P. grunted, nodding his head; Caroline poured a second glass and handed it to him.

"I can get you one," she said.

"Get me one what?" asked J.P. "You already got me a glass of milk." He wiped the milk off his upper lip with the back of his hand. "Thank you," he added.

"I can get you a map of London. Tell me her name, though. She's really pretty."

J.P. stared at her. "Her name's Angela Patricia Galsworthy," he said slowly. "Can you really get one?"

Caroline nodded. "What time is it?"

"Four twenty-seven. *Can you really get one?*"

"Yeah, but I have to hurry. Wait here. Rinse the glasses, okay?"

J.P. nodded, watching her pull on the jacket she had just dropped on a chair. Sometimes Caroline was okay after all.

His sister dashed through the door, and he could hear her feet clattering back down the stairs. He rinsed out the milk glasses, picked up his backpack, took it to his room, and removed his schoolbooks. There was *The Prince and the Pauper;* they had to read two more chapters tonight. That dumb prince was hanging out at London Bridge trying to figure out how to get back to the palace. Where had Angela said London Bridge was? Near the Tower of London. J.P. tried to remember the map he had examined at the bookstore. And what was the name of Angela's street? Church Street? No, it was more interesting than that—more English. Old Church Boulevard? No. Old Church Crescent—that was it.

Old Church Crescent. What a great name for a

street. A perfect place for someone named Angela Galsworthy to live.

J.P. looked around his room. It wasn't a bad room. It wasn't even an unusually messy room; it was cluttered, sure, but it was organized clutter. Every tabletop and desktop was covered with his projects: there was a broken radio, with its disassembled parts carefully arranged so that he could put them back together when he figured out what was malfunctioning; there was a chess set, carefully set up for the game that he'd been conducting with Hope Delafield. J.P. glanced at the few pieces left on the board, trying to remember what dumb move he had made that had caused the checkmate. On a table near the window was an invention he'd been working on for months, with parts of Billy DeVito's broken electric train, which J.P. had found in the trash after Billy got a new train for Christmas; J.P. was trying to hook it all up so that the cars could carry his pencils and paper clips and erasers, and when he flipped a switch at his desk, the supplies would be delivered right to his fingertips while he did his homework.

Now, suddenly, his project with the toy train seemed stupid. The chess game seemed stupid. The broken radio seemed stupid. And messy, and adolescent. And—well, they all seemed so *American*.

His address—West Eighty-Third Street— seemed stupidly American, and his room seemed stupidly American, and his projects seemed stupidly American, and even his *name* seemed stupidly American. J.P. wasn't his real name, of course; it was a nickname made from his initials.

His *real* name was James Priestly Tate. He had always hated it.

But now, suddenly, thinking about his real name—James Priestly Tate—he began to sense that it had a certain ring to it. It sounded like the name of someone who might live on a street called Old Church Crescent. It sounded British.

He looked at himself in the mirror. He raised his chin a bit, tilted his head, and tried to look distinguished. "James Priestly Tate here," he said.

Then he tried to think of something British to add. He remembered the dialogue in *The Prince and the Pauper,* the same dialogue that he had found so boring and so difficult; now it began to seem—

His thoughts were interrupted by the sound of his sister coming through the front door of the apartment. She slammed the door behind her, and he could hear her drop her jacket on the chair once again. Then she came noisily down the hall toward his bedroom.

J.P. turned to Caroline, still holding his chin in the air. "Mannerless wench," he said.

His sister was holding something in her hand. Quickly she thrust it behind her back. "Quit calling me names," she said, "or I'll tear it up."

"I beg your pardon," J.P. said stiffly. "You have my gratitude. At least you have my gratitude if you have a ma—"

"I *do!*" Caroline announced with glee, and she held it out to him. "A map of London! I got it at the travel agency in the next block! Free!"

J.P. snatched it from her. "'Tis somewhat paltry in appearance," he said, "but 'twill do."

"'Twill do, mildew," Caroline said in a singsong

voice. "Quit talking so weird. Now you *owe* me, right?"

"Right," J.P. said, resuming his normal voice as he began to unfold the map. "I do owe you, Caroline." Then he added, "By Jove."

J.P. was working on his math homework in his room after dinner when his mother called from the kitchen.

"Telephone for you, J.P.!"

He had been absorbed in a complicated problem about two cars—a Porsche and a Lamborghini— headed from Geneva to Monte Carlo—in a race, and who would win by how many minutes if they each went so many kilometers per hour; but the Lamborghini got a late start by a few minutes and the Porsche had a mechanical problem along the way, which required two mechanics working for a total price of 1,800 francs, at the going rate of 140 francs per mechanic per hour—so how long did the repair take? You had to figure *that* out, too. J.P.'s math teacher always tried to make the class super interesting, and he usually succeeded; half the class would bring in illustrations that they had drawn for this problem, along with the answer.

He hadn't even heard the telephone ring.

"It's a girl, J.P.," his mom whispered when he got to the kitchen and she handed him the receiver. Caroline looked over from the sink, where she was helping with the dishes, and made a silly face.

J.P. stretched the telephone cord into the living room and sat down on the floor with his back against the wall.

"Hello?" he said nervously. It was the first time a girl had ever called him up. Except his grandmother.

"This is Angela Galsworthy, J.P.," the waterfall voice replied.

"Right. I mean, yeah. I mean, hi."

"Hi. I found your number in the telephone book. I was terribly surprised that it was there: J. Tate. It didn't have the P, just the J."

"Well, actually," J.P. explained, "J. Tate is my mother. Her name is Joanna, but she didn't put her whole name in the book because if some weirdo sees it's a woman, he might make weird phone calls."

"Oh, yes, I see," Angela said politely.

J.P. cringed. He was quite certain she didn't see at all, because she was from London, where there wouldn't be any weirdos, so how could she understand about weird phone calls? He was sorry he had tried to explain the J. Tate in the phone book.

"And, ah, my father lives in Des Moines, so of course we can't have *his* name in the New York directory," J.P. went on. "His name is Herbert," he added.

"Des Moines?" Angela said.

"That's a city. It's nowhere near New York. My parents are divorced."

"Oh," Angela said. "So are mine. I'm here with my father, but my mother is still in London. So my father's name—William—*could* be in the book, but of course we haven't been here long enough. So if you looked for Galsworthy, there might be some, but they wouldn't be me. Though of course there's no reason why you would look for Galsworthy, is there?"

She sounded a little nervous, J.P. realized.

"Well, I might," he said. "If I wanted to ask about a school assignment or something."

"Actually," Angela said, "that's why I rang you up. I thought we might arrange a place to meet to go over the map of London in the morning, before English class." She paused. "You do *have* a map of London, don't you, J.P.?"

"Of course I do." J.P. tried to make himself sound very slightly outraged at the question. "I wouldn't have raised my hand if I didn't."

"No, certainly not," Angela said apologetically. "Shall we meet just before school? Could you come a bit early?"

"I suppose so," J.P. replied. You name the time, he thought. Four a.m.? I could be there at four a.m. No prob.

"At the school library, then, about eight. That should give us time, shouldn't it?"

J.P. agreed, and they said goodbye. He returned the phone to the kitchen, ignored his mother's and sister's questioning looks, and went back to his math. Now when he envisioned the Porsche speeding along the road to Monte Carlo, he envisioned himself in the driver's seat. He pictured the top down, and the wind blowing his hair. Beside him, gazing rapturously into his face, as he fearlessly maneuvered the sleek car down the dangerous, curving mountainous roads (steering with one gloved hand; the other arm was around her shoulders) was Angela Patricia Galsworthy.

Four

This morning Angela had worn her hair differently, J.P. noticed when he entered the school library and saw her sitting there waiting for him.

Usually J.P. paid no attention to hair. He paid no attention to his own, except to have it cut now and then, when his mother insisted; and he *certainly* paid no attention to girls' hair of any sort.

Yet this morning he noticed that Angela Galsworthy was wearing her hair differently. It was not flowing loosely across her shoulders as it had last week, and it was not tied into a thick, gleaming ponytail as it had been yesterday. Today it was folded into a smooth, shimmering knot at the top of her head, exposing her slender neck. And in front of her small pink ears, strands of the golden hair fell in tendrils.

Tendrils. J.P. actually thought that word. He cringed. He blushed and felt his face grow warm.

Angela was smiling at him. "Good morning," she said.

"Hi," J.P. muttered. His shoulders bumped the side of the door as he entered the library, and he tripped over the end of one shoelace. A book toppled from the pile of schoolbooks in his arms. When he knelt to retrieve it from the floor, his calculator fell from his shirt pocket.

On top of everything else, he sneezed. J.P. didn't have a cold, or any allergies that he was aware of. But he sneezed, and he knew that when he sneezed his face got all scrunched up and looked weird, right in full view of Angela Galsworthy. Probably, too, the sneeze left a highly visible drop of something repulsive on the end of his nose; he couldn't reach to wipe it because of the armload of books.

Red-faced, he stumbled and lurched to the library table where she waited. When he sank down, finally, to the chair across from her, its imitation leather seat made a noise that was half hiss, half squeak. Even the furniture was out to humiliate J.P. Tate.

But Angela Patricia Galsworthy only smiled and reached for the folded map that was on top of his stack of books.

"What a perfectly lovely map, J.P.," she said.

He cleared his throat and hoped that his voice wouldn't come out a squawk, as it sometimes did.

"Call me James," he told her.

Mrs. Hunt called J.P. aside as English class ended. He could see Angela linger in the doorway, as if she were waiting for him. Then some of the girls pulled her away and she followed them down the hall toward her next class.

"I want to commend you, J.P.," Mrs. Hunt said. "It was so helpful, having that map. I think the whole class has a much better sense of where the book is taking place now."

"Yeah, well, it was really Angela who showed them. I've never been in London myself."

"I know. And I did thank Angela. But the reason I kept you here was to speak to you about something privately. I didn't want to embarrass you in front of the class."

J.P. looked at her uncomfortably. There was something massively unnerving about a teacher wanting to speak to you privately. He tried to remember if he had handed in all of his book reports.

"I've been noticing the past few days," Mrs. Hunt went on in a concerned voice, "that you seem to be walking a little unsteadily."

"Unsteadily," J.P. repeated.

Mrs. Hunt nodded. "I saw you bump into the doorframe when you entered the classroom this morning. And then you stumbled in the aisle as you went to your seat."

"Stumbled," J.P. said.

"Are you feeling all right?" his teacher asked.

How on earth could he answer that? How could he tell Mrs. Hunt, who was about a hundred and nine years old, that he felt *fine,* that he felt *wonderful,* that he was in love for the first time in his life? And that it was making him walk into doors, and trip over his own feet, and causing his hands to sweat and his ears to itch and his voice to croak and warble? Mrs. Hunt, he should say, my heart is soaring all the time, and I hear music playing, and when Angela Galsworthy smiles my pulse jumps to about three hundred and my nerves all tingle and the temperature of the back of my neck shoots up to about 140 degrees Fahrenheit, and—

"Yeah," J.P. mumbled, looking at the floor. "I feel okay."

Mrs. Hunt stood and gathered her papers from her desk. "Well," she said dubiously, "you're a sensible boy, J.P., and I assume you'll stop in to see the school nurse if you're having problems."

J.P. looked at his watch.

"I do *care* about all my students," Mrs. Hunt went on. "And it worries me when I think something might be wrong. Goodness," she said sadly, "I still remember little Raymond Myerson, and my heart just breaks."

"May I go now?" J.P. asked politely. "I'm going to be late for History."

She nodded. J.P. turned, and bumped the corner of her desk with his hip. He winced. So did Mrs. Hunt.

RAYMOND ALBERT MYERSON

There is no Death! What seems so is transition . . .
H. W. Longfellow

J.P. stood in the hallway outside the science lab and stared at the face in the framed photograph. Raymond Albert Myerson looked like a wimp. Apparently he had been a *rich* wimp, because after his death, his parents had donated the science lab to the Burke-Thaxter School in his memory. Technically, it was called the Myerson Lab; a plaque on the door said so.

The picture had hung there for as long as J.P. could remember—as long as he'd been a student here—but he had never really looked at it before. Now he did.

Raymond wore glasses and had Brillo hair. He stared at the camera without smiling. J.P. squinted, looking more carefully, trying to perceive whether Raymond was already dead when the photograph was taken. His face was so expressionless that J.P. thought he might have been a propped-up corpse. But on careful examination, he saw a tiny blurred spot around the ear, indicating that Raymond Myerson had moved his head a tiny bit just as the camera's shutter was released.

There was no information except his name, the Longfellow quotation, and the dates of Raymond's birth and death in the corner. No explanation of why Raymond Myerson had died at the age of thirteen.

But Mrs. Hunt had thought of Raymond when she talked to J.P. about his own clumsiness. Had Raymond bumped into doorframes and desks too?

"Who's that?" Angela's voice, so close to his shoulder, startled him.

"A dead kid," J.P. replied. Instantly, he hated himself. He couldn't believe he had said something so stupid. He should have said "a *deceased* kid." He wouldn't blame Angela if she stomped away in disgust.

But she continued to stand there, so close he could smell the fragrance of her skin.

"Did you know him?" she asked sadly.

Of course J.P. didn't know Raymond, who had been dead for ten years. He had never even really *looked* at him before, not carefully. And he had no reason to lie to Angela, who had never lied to him.

But the sweet sadness in her voice had affected him in an odd way. The sound of that little tremble as she spoke entered his skin and burrowed into his brain and heart and turned him into a person he had never been. It turned him into a liar.

"He was my cousin," J.P. said reverently, looking straight into the glassy eyes of Raymond Albert Myerson.

Angela gasped slightly. Then she did an incredible thing. She did it right there in an almost public place, the hallway outside the Myerson Lab on the third floor of the Burke-Thaxter School.

She reached over and took J.P.'s hand in hers.

He said nothing. Mentally he ordered his hand to stop perspiring. He continued to stare sadly at the dead wimpy face of Raymond.

"What did he die of?" Angela whispered. "Do you mind talking about it?"

"I don't talk about it to just anyone," J.P. said in a terse, low voice. "But I don't mind telling you. It was a—a—very rare disease."

"Oh," breathed Angela sympathetically.

They stared together at Raymond. Angela's hand was still in his. He thought he felt her squeeze his hand, very slightly. He wasn't *positive,* but it seemed as if a tiny squeeze had taken place, just for a second.

"What was it called?" Angela asked mournfully, in a whisper.

J.P. froze for an instant. He hadn't any idea what had done in poor Raymond Myerson. He could only guess that maybe Raymond, like J.P., had tripped over his own shoelaces and bumped into doorframes.

Angela was waiting for his answer.

"He had triple framosis," J.P. told her.

She gasped. And now—he was certain, this time—she *did* squeeze his hand.

"It runs in families," he whispered to her in a stricken voice, just as a bell rang, the doors at the end of the hall opened, and students began swarming toward them. Angela dropped his hand, but she was looking at him with awe and grief.

"I have to go to gym," J.P. told her in a normal voice. Then he added, more quietly, "I try to keep up my strength by exercising."

"Of course," she said, looking into his eyes with sorrow and with—yes, he was quite sure—it was with love. "I understand," she whispered.

A folded piece of paper dropped onto his desk during Math class just as Angela walked past on her way to the blackboard. "Private" was lettered neatly on the outside in impeccable handwriting.

J.P. unfolded it surreptitiously, in his lap, and glanced down.

"DOES ANYBODY KNOW?" the note said. It was signed simply with her first initial. "A."

J.P. gazed at it. What a wonderfully sophisticated way to sign a note, he thought. What a *British* thing to do. He wondered if Prince Charles signed notes that way, with a simple C. Or maybe P, for Prince.

He looked at the front of the room. Angela had just finished solving the problem on the board. She turned, brushed some chalk dust from the sleeve of her blouse, smiled at the teacher, and headed back to her desk. J.P. followed her with his eyes. Finally she looked back at him quizzically, as if she were waiting for an answer to something.

Oh. He had almost forgotten the question in her note—he'd been so captivated by the signature initial. He read the note again. "DOES ANYBODY KNOW?" Does anybody know *what*, J.P. wondered. Was it a math question? She had done the problem on the board without any trouble. Angela seemed to be quite good at math.

Finally, using his ballpoint pen, J.P. wrote on the same sheet of paper: "KNOW *WHAT?*"

Then he made a large J and folded the note again. On his way to the pencil sharpener, he dropped it in her lap.

Angela read it. He watched her from his desk. Then she looked over at him with a sad, affectionate smile.

When class ended a moment later, she edged her way close to him through the crowd of students heading to the hall. "I meant about your disease," she whispered. "Does anyone else know about your disease?"

"My disease," J.P. repeated stupidly.

Angela stood very close to him and spoke quietly in his ear. "Triple framosis," she whispered. "Does anybody know, besides your family? Is it a secret?"

J.P. cringed inwardly. He hadn't even remembered the name he'd made up for the disease. He knew exactly what he should do at this moment. He should start to laugh. He should laugh *loudly*. He should explain that it was a joke.

But her large sad eyes were so close to him, and they were so sympathetic, and so sweet. There was no way he could laugh, not as long as those eyes were there.

"No," he whispered to her. "No one knows. Only you."

FIVE

ORDINARILY J.P. TOOK A BUS home from school in the afternoons. But today he walked. It was a long walk, through Central Park, from one side of Manhattan to the other, and usually he didn't have time. Usually he was in a hurry to get home so that he could finish some project or do his homework in time to watch TV. But today he needed this extra time for thinking.

He strolled through the park, his book-filled backpack thumping against his shoulders. Around him, people walked either babies, their chubby overalled legs dangling from strollers, or dogs on taut leather leashes. Other people roller-skated, jogged, bicycled, threw Frisbees, sailed past on skateboards, or simply sprawled on the grass or a bench.

J.P. paid no attention to any of them. He was completely absorbed in his own thoughts. His posture and stride took on the rhythm of his thinking.

I am in love with Angela Patricia Galsworthy, he thought, and his shoulders straightened. His steps became jaunty.

And she likes me, I'm sure of it, he thought. He almost tap-danced, almost clicked his heels like Gene Kelly twirling romantically down a city street in an old movie. J.P. grinned.

But, he told himself, the *reason* she likes me — his steps slowed a bit — is because I fibbed. Well, okay, I *lied* to her.

His shoulders slumped and his backpack began to feel heavy, as if it were weighted with boulders.

And now she thinks — J.P.'s walk had turned into a plod; his feet dragged — "*I have a terrible disease!*" he wailed aloud.

"Jeez, kid," a rasping voice said, "don't take it so hard."

Startled, J.P. looked around. The voice had come from a rumpled-looking man who was sitting on a park bench, all alone. Several squirrels scampered around his feet. From a paper bag on his lap, the man drew a handful of peanuts and tossed them to the ground. The squirrels turned instantly into two Super Bowl teams going after a fumble.

The man wasn't watching the squirrels. He was looking at J.P. with interest.

"I'm sorry," J.P. said, embarrassed. "I didn't realize I was talking out loud."

The man didn't bother acknowledging the apology. He tilted his head. He was wearing a filthy baseball cap, and with moist, pink-rimmed eyes he peered up at J.P. from under the visor.

"I got a million diseases myself," he said with a wheeze. "You name it, I got it. But you don't hear *me* complaining."

"You look all right to me," J.P. said skeptically. It wasn't entirely true. The man looked awful;

his shoulders were slumped and his hands shook, though his facial expression was friendly.

"Appearances can't be trusted," the man said. "Name a disease. Go alphabetical."

"What?" J.P. stared at the man.

The man sighed. "A to Z," he explained impatiently. "I got a disease for every letter. Bet you can't match that. Start with A."

The orderliness of the project interested J.P., who was himself a very orderly person. He wandered over to the bench and sat down at the opposite end from the man. The man tossed the last of his peanuts to the head squirrel, the quarterback squirrel, who was instantly sacked by all the others.

"Tell me your name first," the man said, crumpling the empty bag and putting it into his pocket.

"J.P. It's my initials, but it's what everyone calls me."

"Mine's Ralph. Name a disease for A. I got one. Bet you don't."

J.P. thought for a minute. Actually, until today, he had never really had any disease, only chickenpox when he was four. But the man had presented him with a challenge. It seemed more intriguing than a chess game and less troubling than his romantic life at the moment.

"Acne," he announced.

Ralph frowned and leaned forward, squinting with his inflamed eyes to examine J.P.'s face.

J.P. tilted his head to give the man a better view. "See?" he said. "Look at my chin."

Ralph snorted. "*Mild*," he said. "Hardly counts."

"Well," J.P. told him, "you don't have it at all. What's *your* A?"

Ralph lifted his baseball cap briefly, with a flourish. His bald head gleamed in the afternoon sunlight. "Alopecia," he announced. He replaced the cap. "Hair loss," he explained smugly. "Got a B?"

"Lemme think," J.P. told him. "I'm sure I do." He sat still for a minute, thinking about his physical self. Then he looked up. "Body odor," he announced.

Ralph looked at him in disgust. "We're talking serious diseases here and you're coming up with routine puberty items. Listen, kid, I'm going to let you have a point for body odor, but it's a gift on my part and I'm not going to maintain my generosity throughout the entire alphabet. Got it?"

J.P. nodded. "What's *your* B?" he asked, with interest.

"Bursitis," Ralph said. "Fancy name for bum shoulder. On to C."

"Easy," J.P. said. "Common cold." As if to prove the point, he sneezed. Ralph nodded, acknowledging the sneeze as legitimate. "What's yours?" J.P. asked.

"Cataracts. Like a coupla window shades pulled down over the eyes. I can't even see to tell time. You got a watch?"

J.P. nodded and looked at his wrist. "It's four-thirty."

Ralph stood up. "I gotta go. Listen, kid, we only got to C, but like I said, I got a whole alphabet. You wanta admit defeat?"

"You think that's my D?" J.P. asked. "Defeatism?"

Ralph shrugged, coughed, and zipped his jacket. "You got a worse disease for D, tell me tomorrow. I'm here every day. You don't show up, I win by default."

He turned and walked away without saying

goodbye. J.P. watched him go. Then, with a puzzled smile, he turned to head on across the park toward his own home. He found himself chuckling as he walked. He already knew what his D was going to be: dandruff.

"Is Mom home yet?" J.P. asked his sister.

Caroline groaned. "J.P., you ask that every single day. And you *know* she doesn't get home from work till five-thirty. That's not for another half-hour."

He shrugged. "Well, there's always a chance the bank could close early. Maybe if they got held up or something." He grabbed a dishtowel and tied it around the lower half of his face. Then he made a pistol out of his right index finger and pointed it menacingly at Caroline.

"This is a stickup," he said in a low, harsh voice. "Give me everything you've got."

"Ha," Caroline said sarcastically. "I've got three baking potatoes and an uncooked meatloaf that Mom put together this morning. Come on, J.P., help me get dinner started. Find a vegetable in the freezer."

J.P. pulled his gunman's mask off, opened the freezer, and pulled out a package of frozen peas. "These are rich in carbohydrates," he said, tossing the package between his hands. "I probably need extra carbs. I have a whole mess of diseases."

Caroline put the meatloaf and potatoes into the oven and adjusted the temperature. "There," she said. "That'll all be done in an hour. I'll cook the peas later. Or Mom can, after she gets home." Then she looked quizzically at her brother. "What do you mean, you have a whole mess of diseases? You're never sick. You're always bragging that you've never thrown up once in your entire life."

"True," J.P. said. "And I've never had a cavity, either." He opened his mouth wide and aimed his teeth at Caroline. "Perfect alignment, too. Unlike some people."

Caroline made a face at him. The dentist had recently told Mrs. Tate that Caroline needed braces. Now there were a lot of telephone calls back and forth to Iowa, where their father lived, calls having to do with the question of who would pay for Caroline's braces.

Herbert Tate said that he would be responsible for J.P.'s dentistry, since his son had inherited his perfect teeth. And Joanna, his ex-wife, could be in charge of Caroline's, since Caroline had inherited her mother's less-than-perfect ones.

"That's not *fair!*" Joanna Tate had sputtered angrily after she had hung up. "Is it, kids? I ask you: is that fair?"

Caroline and J.P. had both cringed and answered noncommittally. Secretly J.P. thought his mother was right; it *wasn't* fair. But he loved his dad, and he felt a little guilty, being the one with the perfect teeth.

"Maybe I'll inherit his appendix," J.P. had suggested, "and need expensive surgery when it ruptures, the way he did. That way you'd get even."

His mother had frowned at him and shook her head with a sigh, as if appendicitis was not the solution.

Now, with dinner in the oven and their mother due home soon, J.P. and Caroline wandered into the living room of the apartment.

"How's Angela?" Caroline asked. "Did she like the map?"

J.P. nodded. "Yeah," he said. "Thanks."

"Are you going to ask her to the Spring Fling?"

"I forgot all about it," J.P. admitted. "That's right—it's almost May."

The Spring Fling was a custom at the Burke-Thaxter School: a celebration of the season, a time when all the students and teachers wore wild costumes and spent an entire day in wacky enterprises. Usually J.P. avoided the silliness of it as much as he could. Even when his closest friends dressed as rabbits and bumblebees, J.P. always wore his regular school clothes, and he stood on the sidelines, watching, a little embarrassed, each year, as everyone else danced and sang and participated in skits and contests.

He had been vaguely aware of preparations starting. And he remembered that among the older kids, sometimes a boy and girl got together and created matching costumes so that it would be clear they were a couple.

J.P. had never expected to be part of a couple. He had never thought he would *want* to be. J.P. had always, before this, wanted to be the dignified, intelligent loner who stood on the sidelines watching revelry of any sort with a slightly bored, amused look.

Now he was astounded to realize that he wanted to be out there in the middle of things, dancing with Angela Galsworthy, the two of them wearing bright orange butterfly wings.

"Angela won't even know about the Spring Fling," J.P. told his sister, "because she's new. They wouldn't have something like that in London. She'll think it's weird."

Caroline giggled. "It *is* weird. But she'll love it. Anyway, she'll know about it because the new spring calendar came out today. Didn't you get yours?"

She reached into her notebook on the table and pulled out the printed sheet with the Burke-Thaxter logo on top.

"I'll pick mine up tomorrow," J.P. said. He reached for his sister's. "Lemme see yours."

Quickly he glanced down the list of scheduled events: the basketball games, the science fair, the kindergarten trip to the zoo, the parents' meeting, the chess tournament, the—there it was, in a large boxed announcement decorated with computer-drawn flowers — the Spring Fling.

J.P. decided that he would get up his nerve to describe it in more detail to Angela, and ask her to pair up with him in a matching costume.

He took a deep breath. The thought of it was terrifying — it would, after all, be almost a date. His first date. And he was someone who had quite consciously planned never to have a date in his life. Never to fall in love. Never to marry. To devote his life to computer science. To go to MIT and maybe stay there forever, even after graduation, living in one of the labs, coming out only after dark, for food.

He had planned never ever to telephone a girl, except maybe his mother on her birthdays, after she got old.

Now he found his eyes turning toward the telephone on the desk. He thought about calling information to find out Angela's number.

He thought about calling that number.

He thought about asking for Angela. "Ah, is Angela at home, please?" he would say politely to whoever answered. A butler, maybe.

"Is Miss Galsworthy available?" he would say.

He stared at the phone.

Suddenly it rang. He jumped.

Caroline answered it, spoke briefly, then covered the receiver with her hand, turned, and whispered to J.P., "It's for you. It's Angela."

Six

J.P. EXTENDED THE TELEPHONE CORD as far as he could, carried the telephone into the bathroom, and closed the door for privacy. He cleared his throat several times in order to be certain that his voice was working properly, sounding mature, with no squeaks or hiccups in it.

"Hello, hello." He tested his voice, holding his hand over the telephone receiver so that Angela wouldn't hear. He eyed the shower, knowing that if he spoke in that tiled enclosure, there would be, in his voice, a resonant baritone quality that he couldn't achieve anyplace else. But the telephone cord simply wouldn't reach that far.

Finally he took a deep breath and spoke into the receiver. "Hello?" He tried to sound like James Bond: mysterious, sophisticated, and slightly amused.

"Hi, J.P.," Angela replied sweetly. "I hope I'm not interrupting anything."

"No," he reassured her. "My sister and I were just starting to fix dinner because . . ."

Oh, *no.* J.P.'s voice trailed off and his shoulders slumped. He had been about to say "because my mother's not home from work yet." How gross could you get? Probably at the Galsworthy home, a staff of servants fixed dinner.

Fortunately, though, Angela hadn't really been paying attention. She interrupted his unfinished sentence. "J.P.," she said in a concerned whisper, "I know that what you told me today was terribly confidential. And that I shouldn't repeat a bit of it to anybody."

"Right," J.P. agreed. He sighed, with a little smile. He wasn't, actually, paying a lot of attention to her words. He was listening to the way she said them. "Anybody," for example. When J.P. said that word, he pronounced it "ennybuddy." But Angela —well, Angela said something that sounded like "innabawty."

"Innabawty," he said aloud into the telephone, testing his accent. "Innabawty a tall." It sounded so much more refined than his usual "ennybuddy add awl."

"And I wouldn't, I promise," Angela said. "I feel so honored that you confided in me."

J.P. blinked. What exactly was she talking about? He'd been so consumed with passion for her British accent and her sweet, soft voice that he hadn't really listened to the words.

"Excuse me, Angela," he said. "*What's* confidential?"

"You know," she whispered. "Your *disease*."

Oh, that. His disease. He'd almost forgotten the list of diseases. Acne, body odor, common cold— that had sort of been a lie. He had a *slight* cold, maybe—an occasional sneeze—but it might even be an allergy, even though he'd never had an allergy before. Allergies could just sneak up on you and take you by surprise at any moment.

"Which disease?" he asked Angela. He feared the worst. He feared she would say body odor. He glanced at the medicine cabinet where the deodorant, in its pale green container, sat on a shelf behind the mirrored door. He wondered if the phone cord would stretch that far, if he could open the cabinet and reach the deodorant, if he could wedge the telephone receiver against his shoulder and use both hands to remove the cap from the spray can, and reach in under his shirt, and—

"Please, J.P.," Angela said. "You don't need to pretend. Don't be brave. Not with me."

Oh. *That* disease. The fake one. He couldn't even remember its name. J.P. slid down to the floor and sat there, hunched over, with the phone to his ear. He felt miserable.

"Yeah, okay," he said. "I'm not being brave."

"And of course," Angela said, "I understand why you don't want our classmates to know, because you don't want *pity* or anything—"

"Right," J.P. agreed. "No pity."

"But," she was going on, "I know that you don't mind *doctors* knowing about it."

"Doctors?"

"Especially doctors who specialize in genetic disorders. Since it runs in your family."

"Genetic disorders?" J.P. didn't know what she was talking about. Maybe it was her British accent.

"My father is a terribly famous doctor," Angela said. "He specializes in genetic disorders."

"Genetic disorders," J.P. repeated again. He was aware, suddenly, that he sounded like a tape recorder on playback. He was simply repeating everything Angela said.

"I just know he'll be terribly thrilled to meet you," Angela told him cheerfully. "Aren't you fortunate that out of all people you *might* have told, you chose *me*—and I'm the one person in the whole world whose father is a famous doctor who specializes in genetic disorders?"

J.P. stared at the bathroom wall. He lifted the edge of the fuzzy green rug with the toe of his shoe.

Through the closed bathroom door he heard

voices: his sister's and his mother's, talking to each other in the kitchen. He heard the oven door open and close.

"Angela," he said, "I have to go."

"I understand," she said sympathetically. "You're stunned."

"I'm stunned," J.P. agreed.

"I'll ring off, then," she said. "But let me just tell you quickly, first, that the obvious time for you to meet my father is May first, at school."

"May first? Why is that obvious?" J.P. remembered, suddenly, that he had intended to ask Angela to be his partner for the Spring Fling. "Do you know about the Spring Fling, Angela?"

"I've just been hearing about it from the girls at school," Angela said, "and it sounds like such fun. And parents are invited, so I'm sure my father will be terribly keen on coming.

"And of course," she went on, "he can meet your cousin's family at the same time."

J.P. blinked. All of his cousins lived in the Midwest. He hardly ever saw them. One of his girl cousins was a gymnastics champion in Iowa. Or Ohio. Or Idaho, maybe. One of those vowel states.

"My cousin's family?" he said, puzzled, to Angela.

"The Myersons," she said. "J.P., didn't you know they were coming? It's right there in the school calendar — that's how I knew."

"I really have to hang up," J.P. said miserably. And he did.

There it was, wedged in between the information about the chess tournament and the kindergarten zoo trip. He hadn't even noticed it. The Myersons were going to be there, to rededicate the Myerson Lab and to donate more equipment in memory of their kid, Raymond. It was the tenth anniversary of his death, so they were buying a batch of new microscopes.

"J.P.," his mother said, "can't you put that down during dinner? Let's try to be civilized, okay? Even though it's just meatloaf."

J.P. folded the school calendar and laid it on his lap. He took a bite of meatloaf.

"Spring Fling's coming, Mom," Caroline explained. "And J.P. never bothered about it before because it seemed too silly. But now he has this girl, so he has to pay attention to stuff like this."

J.P. glared at his sister. But Caroline wasn't needling him. She really was only explaining to their mother.

"I wish I didn't have to work that day," Joanna Tate said. "I remember that one year I got to go to your Spring Fling, and it was really fun. But this year I have to work. I took too many days off when I had the flu in February."

"Are Angela's parents coming, J.P.?" Caroline asked.

J.P. sighed, and mashed some margarine into his baked potato. "Her parents are divorced," he said. "And she's here in New York with her father." He sighed again. "And yes," he went on, "her father is coming."

Caroline looked up eagerly. "Is her father handsome? I bet he is, because she's so pretty. And he's probably just the right age. Mom—"

Joanna Tate shook her head firmly. "No," she

said. "Absolutely not, Caroline. I am *not* interested. And I doubt if he is, either."

Caroline made a face and turned her attention back to her meatloaf.

"J.P.?" his mother asked. "Are you okay?" She looked at him with concern.

"Me? Yeah."

His mother reached across the table and touched his forehead. "You're so preoccupied tonight," she said. "Do you have a fever? You don't feel sick, do you?"

J.P. nudged her hand away. "I'm fine," he muttered.

"The chess tournament's coming up, Mom," Caroline pointed out. "So J.P. has a lot to think about. Also," she added. "Don't forget. He's in love."

And in trouble, J.P. thought, though he didn't say it aloud. Serious trouble.

SEVEN

Just one week until the Spring Fling, and the day of the Spring Fling would also be the—

day of the chess tournament finals, and J.P. had not been thinking about chess, not been playing practice games, not been reading chess magazines. In the old days—before Angela—J.P. frequently, and secretly, tried out a Russian accent, pretending to himself that he was Boris Spassky, former Soviet champion. Now the only accent he used was his fake James Bond, a vaguely Scottish-British affectation, which made him feel glamorous, dangerous, and desirable as long as he avoided looking into a mirror. He would use his James Bond accent in one week, on the day of the Spring Fling when he would be forced to meet—

Angela's father, Dr. Galsworthy, who would probably, as they shook hands, be secretly trying to feel his pulse. Before that day, just one week from now, J.P. would have to think of methods to create symptoms of triple framosis. He knew that he could trip over his feet and walk into doors, because he did that all the time anyway. But it wouldn't be enough, not for a distinguished British specialist in genetic disorders. J.P. would have to create a pale complexion, perhaps a low-grade fever, a racing pulse, all of those things probably familiar symptoms to the family of—

Raymond Myerson, whose parents, whom he had never met and never seen and never really even heard of until the day he read the plaque outside of the science lab, would be visiting the Burke-Thaxter School on the day of the Spring Fling. J.P. would have to figure out how to deal with that. He knew that the only answer might be moving to a different state and changing his identity. He wondered how excruciating it would be to burn off his fingerprints with acid. He wondered whether, after he had eaten away his fingertips and changed his facial features by plastic surgery and taken a new identity and moved to a small town in North Dakota, he would be able to get in touch with a very few selected people who would not give him away. His mother, for one. His father, in Des Moines. And maybe, just maybe—

Angela Patricia Galsworthy, who, only a few minutes before (J.P. grinned, remembering) had agreed to be his partner on the day of the Spring Fling.

He had asked her just as school ended, just as all the kids were crowding through the front doors of the building, calling to each other, shoving and poking and laughing. Asking her there, in the crowd, in the confusion, would have given him a chance to fade away and disappear, if she had said no.

But she had said yes. And then, smiling, she had waved to him and dashed off down the steps with some girls from their class.

And so, despite his other worries, and his very

real fear that he wouldn't adjust well in North Dakota and that burning off his fingerprints with acid would so reduce the sensitivity of his fingers that he would never ever, if he wanted to, be able to read Braille, use an abacus, or play the violin—despite all of those concerns, J.P.'s steps were light and his shoulders straight as he headed home, through the park.

Because Angela had said yes.

Ralph was there, on the same bench, wearing today a pair of mottled green-and-brown camouflage trousers and a sweatshirt that said NEW ENG-LAND PATRIOTS. Even J.P., who ordinarily cared very little about clothes, could see that the mix-and-match was not successful.

Ralph looked up matter-of-factly, as if he had been expecting J.P., and said, "So, kid. What's your D?"

J.P. had prepared. He was planning to say dandruff. If Ralph wanted proof, he was planning to lean his head over Ralph's lap and run his fingers through his hair. The camouflage pants might be a hindrance. But J.P. really *did* have dandruff, and he was certain it would show.

But he found, when he began to speak, to answer Ralph, that he didn't say dandruff. Instead he said, to his own surprise, "Deceitfulness."

Ralph stared at him with a long, squinting, thoughtful look. Finally he said, "We'll do character flaws next. Right now we're dealing in the strictly physical. I'll ask you again: What's your D?"

"Dandruff," J.P. replied, with a sigh, and Ralph nodded, accepting the answer.

"What's yours?" J.P. asked.

"Huh?"

"I said, 'What's yours?' What's your D, Ralph?" J.P. repeated.

"What say?" Ralph cupped one hand behind his ear, tilting his baseball cap a bit.

J.P. grinned. "WHAT'S YOUR D?" he bellowed.

"Deafness," Ralph said, and adjusted his cap.

"Why don't you get a hearing aid? This kid at school, Kevin Kerrigan, has a hearing aid, and he uses it like a *weapon*." J.P. glowered, thinking about Kevin Kerrigan, who was such a pain.

Ralph shrugged. "Maybe if it gets worse," he said. "Right now it comes and goes. Now for E. Gimme your E."

J.P. hadn't thought ahead to E. But, thinking quickly, he remembered back to the pre-Angela days, back when he was still paying a lot of attention to his chess game. He remembered those hours of sitting and staring at the chess pieces, occasionally rubbing his eyes with weariness and with —

"Eyestrain," he announced to Ralph.

Ralph made a face, twisting his mouth into a skeptical look. "*Eyestrain?*" he asked dubiously.

"And earwax," J.P. added quickly. "Excessive earwax. What's *your* E, Ralph?" he asked politely, hoping to divert Ralph's attention away from his own E, which even J.P. had to admit was not as well thought-out as it might have been.

"Emphysema," Ralph muttered gloomily. "Forty years of cigarettes. Now I can't even breathe. Listen." He drew a deep breath, or tried to, and it ended in a wet, choking cough. J.P. could hear the gasping wheeze behind Ralph's breathing. He cringed. He had already, long ago, decided never to smoke. Now he renewed that decision.

"We're up to F," he said to Ralph, who was still trying to stop coughing.

Ralph nodded, slapping his hand against his knee as he struggled to catch his breath. "You go," he said.

"*Framosis*," J.P. announced in a stricken voice. Then he continued, "Also, fabrication and fraud."

"I *told* you," Ralph said impatiently, when he got his breath and his voice back, "character flaws are a different competition. And what are you talking about, framosis?"

"Triple framosis," J.P. muttered.

"No such thing. You got an F, or not?"

J.P. sighed. If even an old bum on a park bench knew that there wasn't such a thing as triple framosis, how on earth would he fool Angela's father, the famous doctor?

"Let's get on the ball here, kid. I asked you: You got an F?"

"Facial hair?" J.P. suggested. "I've got a little if you look close."

"Listen," Ralph said wearily, "I like you, kid, so I'm going to help you out a little here. Facial hair is not an affliction. It's simply a condition of the male half of the human species, sometimes even the female half as well. I had an aunt once who had a full mustache. And my wife, when I had one, did an occasional pluck in the chin area. It's no disease, kid.

"But lemme ask you this: Do you ever see little spots drifting across your line of vision? Like pieces of dust inside your eyeball?"

J.P. thought about it. He looked up at the sky; and there, against the expanse of blue, as J.P. stared, a small spot flickered across and disappeared. "Yeah," he said in surprise to Ralph. "I just saw one."

Ralph nodded. "Okay. You got floaters. Most people do. Won't kill you, won't make you blind. But floaters are a legitimate F. I got 'em myself."

He stood up, smoothed his Patriots sweatshirt, and stretched. "I've got you beat on F," he said, "because I suffer from flat feet and flatulence both. But you're doing okay, kid. You're keeping up, now that you got the hang of it. I'll see you Monday. We'll be on G then."

He turned and began to walk away. Then he stopped and looked back at J.P. "Listen," he said, "about the character flaws. Yours seem to be falling into a pattern, see. For G, you're gonna wanta say *guile*. It goes with that other stuff: deceitfulness and fraud. But the thing is, kid, you don't hafta have character flaws like that. That's why I don't sympathize with 'em, see?"

Ralph turned again and shuffled off along the path while J.P. watched. He looked back one more time and called, "Floaters, you're stuck with those. No getting rid of floaters!"

He waved briefly and disappeared down the curving path.

EIGHT

J.P. STOOD ALONE in front of the science lab, staring gloomily at the photograph of Raymond Myerson. The hallway was empty. It was lunchtime, and everyone else was in the cafeteria. But J.P. hadn't felt like eating.

"This is all your fault, Myerson," he muttered.

Raymond Myerson stared back with glassy eyes.

"You turned me into a liar and a cheat," J.P. explained to the photograph. "And my very first love affair is going to end disastrously because of it.

"Because I'm guileful," he added. He hadn't even

known what the word "guile" meant when his friend Ralph had used it the previous afternoon. He had gone home immediately and looked it up in the dictionary.

"'Treachery and deceitful cunning,'" J.P. had read aloud from the dictionary in his bedroom. "*Right.* That's me, all right!" He threw the dictionary across the room in despair. It had still been lying there on the floor, next to his abandoned electric-train project, when he left for school this morning.

"James?" Angela's soft voice was shy. She had come up behind him quietly in the deserted hall. J.P. jumped, startled.

"I'm sorry to bother you, especially when you're thinking about your cousin," she said politely. "But I looked for you in the cafeteria and you weren't there."

"I wasn't hungry."

Angela caught her breath. "I'm so sorry," she whispered sympathetically. J.P. cringed, realizing that she was, in her mind, listing "lack of appetite," or even "anorexia," as a symptom of his terrible disease.

"I thought we might get together to plan our costumes for the Spring Fling," Angela suggested. "Lindsay and Antonio are going to be robins. They're making wings and tails out of cardboard, and they're going to have red breasts."

J.P. could feel his face begin to turn crimson. Hearing anyone say the word "breasts" aloud always made his face redden, but to hear *Angela* say it, even if she was talking about *robins*—well, J.P.'s face became warmer and pinker than usual.

But she hadn't noticed. She hadn't even noticed, J.P. realized, that she had said that word "breasts" aloud. She just continued talking very cheerfully.

"And Mr. Goldfine says that because of his name he's going to be a goldfinch. He has some bright yellow trousers, he says, that he bought once for a trip to the Caribbean, and he's going to get a yellow shirt to go with them, and then he'll paint some black trim on the shirt, and wear a black mask, because a goldfinch has a black mask across its face. Does everyone have to do *birds,* James? Because the good birds all seem to be taken."

J.P. shook his head. "It just has to be connected

to spring somehow," he said. "That's the only rule. Lots of people do flowers and stuff."

Angela looked at her watch. "We still have ten minutes before class starts," she said. "Let's sit down in here and think." She opened the door to the empty science lab—the Myerson Lab—and J.P. followed her inside.

"Spring," she mused, after she had settled herself on one of the lab stools.

"Spring," J.P. replied. Once again he was aware of his tendency to repeat everything that Angela said. There was a name for that, he recalled: *echolalia.* He had read about it once. J.P. gulped, thinking of it. Echolalia was a symptom of schizophrenia.

"'In spring a young man's fancy lightly turns to thoughts of love,'" Angela said suddenly, with a bashful smile. "That's Tennyson," she explained.

Hearing Angela say the word "love" was *almost* as embarrassing as hearing her say "breasts." Not quite, but almost. J.P. tried frantically to change the subject. "You'd think a guy named Tennyson would write about tennis," he said. "People's thoughts turn to tennis in the spring."

"Perhaps we could dress as tennis rackets," Angela suggested. "But I can't for the life of me imagine how to do it."

"Tennis rackets," J.P. said, thinking. Echolalia again.

"Hey, Angela!" he said suddenly. "How about golf! People's thoughts turn to golf in the spring!"

"Golf?" Angela said. "If we can't dress as tennis rackets, how on *earth* could we dress as golf clubs?"

"Not clubs, Angela. *Bags!* Golf bags! What do you think? It'd be original! In all the years I've been going to Spring Fling, no one's ever dressed as a golf bag!"

"*Golf bags?*" Angela's eyes were wide and skeptical.

"Look," J.P. said. His voice was excited now. *He* was excited. He was certain that nobody had *ever* worn a golf bag costume to Spring Fling. "You and I: we're both pretty ski—" He hesitated. He had been about to say "skinny," but he realized that might seem insulting to Angela. "We're both slender," he said. Angela nodded, agreeing with him.

"I bet anything we could each fit into a golf

bag," he told her. "All we have to do is cut eyeholes and armholes."

"But where would we get golf bags?" Angela asked. "They're terribly expensive. I know my father would never—"

"Easy!" J.P. said, elated that he had thought of such a unique idea. "Near where I live, on the West Side, there's a crummy old thrift shop. It's where winos and bag people buy their winter coats? I get electronic stuff there, broken clocks and radios to fool around with. Once my mom got an old clothes basket there, for a quarter, and she painted it green to match the rug, and she keeps magazines in it, in the bathroom, so now if you're—"

He stopped, suddenly, hideously embarrassed once again, this time because he had begun talking about bathrooms in front of Angela.

But Angela was listening with interest. "Do they have golf bags there?" she asked.

J.P. nodded. "Always. In the back there are *always* old golf bags. They never sell them, because the people in the store aren't the kind of people who play golf. So there's always a pile of old golf bags. There are leather ones, or plaid—"

"I want to be plaid," Angela said, her eyes dancing with anticipation. "Are they expensive, do you think?"

J.P. shook his head. "They'll probably pay us to take a couple of them away," he told her. "You want to come home with me after school today, and check it out?"

She nodded, and J.P.'s heart soared with astonishment, passion, and success.

Walking through Central Park after school, the beautiful Angela Patricia Galsworthy by his side, J.P. nodded a greeting to his oddly dressed friend Ralph, who was on his usual bench.

Ralph raised an eyebrow at J.P. "G for gingivitis," he announced as J.P. neared the bench. "Gum disease. I lost all my teeth to gingivitis years ago. These here are fake." He grinned an exaggerated grin, to show J.P. his dentures.

J.P. grinned back. He took a deep breath and

reached for Angela's hand. Never before in his entire life had he intentionally taken a girl's hand, not since the time he grabbed his little sister by the wrist when she was three and had almost run out into the traffic-filled street on Central Park West.

But today he took Angela's hand, and she did not draw hers back.

"Goose bumps," he said happily to Ralph, and continued on through the park with Angela's hand in his.

The little shop on upper Broadway, not far from the Tate apartment, was called Attic Treasures, but the word "treasures," J.P. thought, was an exaggeration; and "attic" may have been, too. What it was, was "basement junk." Stuff that the trash guy hadn't picked up yet.

He and Angela stopped on the sidewalk and peered through the grimy windows.

"Look!" J.P. said, pointing. "A whole set of old dentist's tools. I may buy that sometime. It's probably expensive, though."

Angela glanced, with a look of distaste, around

the dusty collection of things that were visible through the window. "It's terribly musty," she said.

"Think what you could *do* with dentist's tools," J.P. said blissfully.

Angela shuddered. Finally she said, "I see a pretty dish over there. But it has a crack down the middle."

"Yeah," J.P. said happily. "A lot of the stuff's broken. That's when you can really get a bargain, when it's broken. I got a toaster once for forty cents. Heck, the *parts* were worth more than that."

Angela looked skeptical. But she followed gamely when J.P. pushed open the door and went inside.

"Mr. Mudgett?" J.P. called. "Anybody home?"

From the back of the dimly lit, cluttered room came a fluttering sound as some papers had fallen from the top of a high stack. Behind them, the figure of a tall, bald man arose. He squinted toward J.P. and Angela, adjusting his metal-rimmed glasses across the bridge of a long, rather crooked nose. He smiled.

"James," he said. "Welcome. I'm afraid I was dozing. I set out to look through these old piles of sheet music. Look here, I have 'In a Little Spanish Town' in my hand, still. That's 1926, imagine that. You weren't even born, James. Your *mother* wasn't born. And I myself was just a boy. Coolidge was president. Did you know that, James? Who was president in 1926?"

J.P. shook his head. "I would've guessed Teddy Roosevelt, if it was a quiz show," he admitted.

Mr. Mudgett hummed a few bars of "In a Little Spanish Town"; he set the piece of music back on a precariously tall stack, and dusted it with the side of his hand.

"Coolidge was president, Jimmy Walker was mayor of New York, Pius the Eleventh was pope, and Bubbling Over won the Kentucky Derby," he murmured. "Not a bad year, 1926." Then he turned toward J.P. and Angela again. "Who's your friend, James?" he asked politely, readjusting his glasses.

J.P. introduced Angela to Mr. Mudgett. The old man tilted his head with interest as he listened to her accent.

"British," he said. "I don't know a single thing that happened in Great Britain in 1926, I'm afraid. Do you?"

Angela shook her head. "I'm sorry," she told him.

"What can I do for you today, James?" Mr. Mudgett asked.

J.P. pointed toward the door that obviously led to a back room. "I remembered that you had a whole bunch of old golf bags out there. And Angela and I—"

"Bobby Jones won the U.S. Open in 1926," Mr. Mudgett announced happily. "But Walter Hagen took the PGA tournament that year.

"Not a bad year, 1926, except for the economy," he said to himself. Then he turned again to J.P. "Go take a look, you and your friend. Special this week on golf bags. Any two for a dollar."

Angela followed J.P. to the back room. Behind them, they could hear Mr. Mudgett singing to himself and could hear the shuffling of his feet on the wooden floor. He was dancing, too.

"*In,*" Mr. Mudgett sang with emphasis, "da da da—a little Spanish *town*—da da da—"

NINE

"WELL, J.P.," HIS MOTHER said at dinner that night, "I really have to hand it to you. You're one of a kind. A true original."

"*Really,* J.P.," his sister, Caroline, said, with admiration in her voice.

J.P. beamed and reached for another helping of chicken. It was his finest hour.

For one thing, Angela Patricia Galsworthy was actually there, actually sitting across the table, in the Tates' kitchen, eating dinner with them as if it were not the most surprising event in the world. Mrs. Tate had said sure, when J.P. asked; and Angela's father had said sure, when Angela called (although J.P. was quite certain that a distinguished British doctor wouldn't say "sure"; he probably had said, "By all means"—or maybe "Righto").

And in addition, J.P. and Angela were going to have the most original, most startling costumes that had ever represented spring at the Burke-Thaxter School.

The two golf bags were propped up against the wall in the living room. J.P.'s was dark green, and Angela's was red plaid. They were ready, at last, for the Spring Fling, though it had not been an easy afternoon.

First, while Caroline watched with fascination, J.P. had laid both golf bags on the living room rug.

"Which one do you want, Angela?" he had asked politely.

"The red plaid, I think," Angela said. "If that's all right with you, of course, James," she added. Caroline had put her hand to her mouth and giggled.

No one had ever *ever* said "if that's all right with you, of course, James" to her brother before.

"That's just fine," J.P. said. "Okay, climb in and let's see how it fits."

"Which way?" Angela asked, looking at the golf bag with a frown. "Head or feet first?"

"Head," J.P. directed. "Then I'll be able to tell where to put the eyeholes."

Angela knelt at the open end of the bag and peered in apprehensively. Then she took a deep breath, lay flat on the rug, and began to wiggle into the bag headfirst.

"You look like a snake going into a hole!" Caroline called.

"It's terribly dark in here!" Angela's voice was muffled. Her shoulders had disappeared; soon her arms, too, were gone. She had had to hold them tightly to her sides in order to fit into the bag. The hem of her skirt disappeared. Then her knees, too, were gone. Finally nothing showed of Angela except her knee socks and shoes.

"Is that as far as you can go?" called J.P.

"Yes!" Angela's muffled voice replied.

"Okay, stand up!" J.P. called.

There was a silence. Then Angela called back, "Stand up?"

"Yeah, so I can find the place for eyeholes!"

Silence. Angela's feet wiggled, as if she were trying to swim.

Caroline whispered to her brother. "J.P., she can't stand up! She can't *bend!*"

"Why are you whispering?" J.P. whispered back.

"I don't know. Is she all right? Why isn't she saying anything?"

Angela's feet wiggled again.

"Angela, I'm going to stand you up, okay?" J.P. called into the bag.

"Okay, I guess." The voice sounded a long distance away, and not very happy.

"Help me, Caroline," J.P. directed. Together they lifted the golf bag, with Angela inside, into a standing position.

Tentatively Angela moved her feet. She walked a couple of short steps across the living room.

"Remember that old TV commercial, J.P.? The one with the dancing cigars?" Caroline whispered.

J.P. was watching the golf bag with interest. "Yeah," he said. "It looks a lot like that, doesn't it?

"Angela!" he called. "Try a dance step!"

But Angela's feet had stopped moving. She planted them both resolutely on the Tates' living room rug.

"Help!" she called.

"Help with what?" J.P. called back into the plaid canvas of the bag.

"Get me out!" Angela wailed. "I can't breathe!"

J.P. sighed. "I knew there was going to be a flaw," he said unhappily.

Together he and Caroline lifted the golf bag off of Angela, exposing her knees, then her skirt, then her arms, and finally her shoulders and head. Her blond hair was coated with feathers of dust and her forehead glowed with perspiration.

Angela took a deep breath, and then another. "I have claustrophobia," she said. "I never knew it before."

Claustrophobia, J.P. thought. That was an *excellent* C. Much better than common cold. Aloud, he said, "It's not going to work that way, even with eyeholes. Lemme try it feet first."

He lay on the floor at the end of the green bag, and began to slither in, as Angela and Caroline watched.

J.P. eyed the two bags as he finished the ice cream his mother had served for dessert. He and Angela and Caroline had worked all afternoon on them, and they were just about perfect now. They had carefully removed each bottom, so that they could now stand inside the bags with their heads emerging from one end and their feet from the other. They had cut armholes. It was tough to slither into the bag and poke your arms into the holes, but after you got the hang of it, it could be done. And once you were inside, the bag didn't slip. At first that had been a problem. But J.P. had invented and installed shoulder straps, and now the golf bags stayed in place.

They could walk, wearing the bags, if they took

short steps. They couldn't sit or bend, of course. But that didn't seem important. They could breathe, which *was* important.

"How will we dance, James?" Angela had asked, as she practiced mincing steps across the living room, her head visible at the top of the red plaid bag, her shoes visible at the bottom. "Didn't you tell me that there's dancing at the Spring Fling?"

J.P., wearing the green bag, took a few tiny dance steps. "We'll start a new fad," he suggested. "The Golf Bag Dance. Everybody at Burke-Thaxter will be doing it by the end of the Spring Fling." He hummed for a moment, getting the melody right. Then he sang, and moved his feet in the tiny steps, which were the only steps possible when you were wearing a golf bag.

"*In*, da da da," J.P. sang, "a little Spanish *town*, da da da . . ."

Angela danced mincingly, in her bag, over to where he was, and took his hand. Neither of them knew any more lyrics to the 1926 song, but they sang the first line over and over, as they did the Golf Bag Dance together.

Caroline watched rapturously. "I envy you guys," she said with a sigh. "I'm just wearing my dumb old bumblebee outfit from last year. And one antenna's all bent."

But by morning, J.P.'s elation had disappeared. He left for school early and walked across the park instead of taking the bus. He needed the time to think.

The night before, when it was time for Angela to leave, when her father had rung the doorbell and was waiting for her downstairs—he hadn't wanted to come up because he was double-parked—Angela had thanked Mrs. Tate politely for the dinner. She had said goodbye cheerfully to Caroline. She had grinned at the two golf bags standing like huge red and green cocoons against the wall.

Then she had said, "Come downstairs with me, would you, J.P.? Just for a minute?"

He had planned to walk her down anyway. But when she asked, J.P.'s heart soared. That's how he thought of it, though he knew it was a cliché from a crummy romance novel. His heart soared. His heart had been soaring a lot lately.

His heart soared this time because he was quite certain that Angela Patricia Galsworthy was going to kiss him good night. All the way down the stairs from the Tate apartment, surreptitiously, so that Angela, in front of him, couldn't see, J.P. practiced moving his lips around, hoping to find what felt like the right position for kissing. Although he had never kissed a girl before, J.P. was sure that he would *feel* the right position when he came to it.

At the bottom of the stairs, Angela turned to him.

But she didn't kiss him at all. Instead she said quickly, "I just wanted to say to you, James, that I think you're *terribly* brave."

"Brave?" His lips, readied for kissing, had trouble forming the word.

"To do all of this — the golf bags and all — with your illness," Angela whispered. "*Terribly* brave," she had said again, passionately, and then ran out to where her father's car was waiting.

Now, trudging through the park with slumped shoulders, J.P. wondered once more how he had gotten into such a mess.

It startled him that Ralph was there, on the bench. J.P. looked at him in surprise. He had seen Ralph only in the afternoons, and it had never occurred to him that anyone would sit in Central Park all day, beginning at—J.P. looked at his watch—seven forty-five a.m.

Ralph observed J.P.'s surprise. "Insomnia," he explained. "That's my I. But we're really only at H. Mine's halitosis. Don't ever get too close to me, not till I've popped a Cert." He grinned and unwrapped a roll of breath mints.

"What's your H?" Ralph asked cheerfully.

J.P. thought. My H, he thought. Hypocrisy, that's what it is. I'm the world's biggest hypocrite.

But he knew that Ralph wouldn't accept that as his H. It wasn't physical—even though (J.P. could feel it) he had decidedly physical symptoms. A pain in his chest and a spasmodic twitching of his whole upper body.

He looked at Ralph and sighed. "Heartburn," he announced. "And hiccups."

Then he trudged disconsolately on to school.

Ten

J.P. GLANCED AT THE BLACKBOARD when he entered English class. Each day Mrs. Hunt put a different quotation on the board, and she gave a little extra credit to whichever class member could identify the source of the quotation.

J.P. had been pretty successful at many of them, though he never got the ones that came from movie stars or musicians, not even the ones from old Beatles songs, which everyone else in the whole world seemed to know.

But just last month he had been the only one

in the class to identify "I LIKE THE MOMENT WHEN I BREAK A MAN'S EGO."

He had even been the only member of the *chess* club to identify that one, which came from Bobby Fischer, the famous chess player. J.P. wasn't certain that he agreed with the philosophy, though he had been happy to get the extra credit from Mrs. Hunt.

Today he didn't recognize the source of the quotation, but glumly he realized, after reading it, that he did agree with what it said.

> *"Oh, what a tangled web we weave*
> *When first we practice to deceive!"*

It was Angela who raised her hand for the extra credit today. "That's Sir Walter Scott," she said, and Mrs. Hunt beamed at her.

"He was British," Angela explained to the class. "And I studied him at school in London last year. That's how I knew."

J.P. bent his head toward *The Prince and the Pauper* as the whole class turned to the chapter they were discussing. But the quotation on the board stayed with him. J.P. had a phenomenal memory. Whatever he saw, whatever he heard, whatever he read, he remembered.

That was why he got good grades in school, why he was a terrific chess player, why he would always know, from now on—ever since yesterday—that Coolidge had been president, Jimmy Walker had been mayor, Pius the Eleventh had been pope, and Bubbling Over had won the Kentucky Derby in 1926.

And now, he knew, he would always remember what Sir Walter Scott had said about deceit.

He sighed, turned the page in his book, and wished devoutly that he were a prince, or a pauper, or a president or a pope, even—anyone at all except James Priestly Tate.

"J.P.?"

"What?" J.P. turned at the door to Mrs. Hunt's classroom. English class had ended, and he had lingered in the doorway, hoping to walk with Angela to History, maybe even carrying her schoolbooks the way boys did in old magazines and Andy Hardy movies. But she had dashed on ahead, giggling, with some girlfriends.

It was red-haired Hope Delafield who was standing by his side waiting to say something to him. Good old Dopey Hopie. Hope wasn't really a dope; in fact, she was the best girl chess player in the school. But her parents should have known when they *named* her that she would be nicknamed Dopey in third grade. Parents should always think about stuff like that when they name a kid, J.P. thought for about the sixty-seventh time. Look what happened to Elvis, for example; he got stuck with the nickname Pelvis, and even though he made a fortune being Elvis the Pelvis, J.P. suspected that he probably had secretly wished all his life to be named something like Elmore, instead.

Hope's freckled face was distressed. "I just wanted to tell you that I lost to Kevin in the semi-finals of the chess tournament," she said gloomily. "We played after school yesterday. I thought you'd be there to watch."

Darn. Even with his phenomenal memory, J.P. had forgotten the Kerrigan-Delafield match. He had meant to go and watch. But he had been sidetracked by Angela and the golf bags.

"How did you lose to Kerrigan? You're usually better than he is, Hope," J.P. said. "Even when he turns off his hearing aid. You're better than I am at ignoring distractions."

Hope sighed. "Well, I blew it. I was white, and I tried a queen's pawn opening. Pawn to queen four?"

J.P. nodded with interest, picturing the chess board in his mind. "What defense did he use?" he asked Hope.

"I think it's called the Gruenfeld Defense. Knight to king's bishop three was his next move."

J.P. chuckled. "I didn't think old Kerrigan was that smart. So you ended up losing. Rats, Hope. I thought you'd beat him."

She smiled ruefully. "Maybe next time. Anyway, J.P., I thought it would be you and me playing against each other for the championship. But now you have to play him. Have you been practicing?"

"Of course," J.P. lied. I've been practicing how to dance while wearing a golf bag, he admitted to himself. I've been practicing how to arrange my lips to kiss Angela Galsworthy. Of *course* I've been practicing.

"The final match is during the Spring Fling," Hope reminded him tentatively.

"Yeah, I know. It is every year."

"Are you, ah, going *with* anyone to the Spring Fling?"

J.P. looked at her. Last year he hadn't gone with Hope, actually, to the Spring Fling. But she and he had been two of the very few who hadn't worn costumes. They had spent a lot of time standing on the sidelines together. So it almost seemed as if they had been a couple.

He felt bad when he responded to her question. "Yeah," he said. "I'm going with Angela."

Hope nodded and shrugged and smiled, the way she always did when people called her Dopey Hopie. As if she understood that they liked her anyway, that they didn't mean it as an insult. "Well," she said, "I hope you beat Kevin in the finals. You've been champion for three years now. I'll be there rooting for you.

"Spring Fling's next week, you know," she

reminded him as they walked on to History class together. "You'd better start brushing up on the middle game after a single queen's pawn opening. And listen, J.P., here's something else.

"Kevin's got his friends and his brother all lined up. I heard them talking. They're going to do a whole lot of distracting stuff. Blowing their noses, and sneezing, and burping, and scratching mosquito bites—that kind of stuff. Nothing illegal. Nothing they can get thrown out of the room for, just stuff to make you lose your concentration."

J.P. nodded as they entered the classroom, where the teacher was already pulling down a large pink map of the Roman Empire from the roller above the blackboard. He took his seat quickly and tried very hard to think about the conquest of Gaul. In his mind, though, J.P. was seeing knights and bishops marching across a checkered landscape, knocking helpless pawns aside as they advanced.

"Mom," J.P. asked that evening after dinner, "you know how to knit, right?"

His mother looked at him in surprise. "Of

course I know how to knit. Who do you think made you that heavy brown crewneck sweater you like so much?"

"Yeah, right. I forgot."

"Why?"

"Well, I was wondering how long it would take you to knit a—what do you call those things that babies wear on their feet?"

Caroline looked up from the magazine she was reading. "Booties," she said.

J.P. made a face. What a gross word: "booties." He forced himself to say it, nevertheless. "How long would it take you to knit a baby bootie?"

"Let me think," Joanna Tate said. "I made a pair of baby booties when Dottie Sorenson had her baby, and I guess it took me about—"

J.P. interrupted her. "I don't mean a pair. How long would it take to knit just one bootie?"

His mother stared at him with a puzzled frown. "Do you know someone with a one-legged baby, J.P.?"

"It's just an academic question."

Joanna Tate shrugged and thought for a minute. "An hour," she said, finally. "I could knit one baby bootie in one hour. No fancy stuff or frills, though. Just straightforward baby bootie."

"Regardless of size?"

Caroline had set her magazine completely aside and was listening avidly. "J.P.!" she said. "Tell the truth. Do you know somebody who's *pregnant?*"

"Mom!" J.P. exploded. "Does she have to eavesdrop on every single conversation in the whole world?"

"No," his mother said mildly. "Of course she doesn't. Quit eavesdropping, Caroline. Read your magazine." Her voice dropped slightly and became just as eager as Caroline's. "Now, tell the truth, J.P. Do you know somebody who's pregnant?"

"Forget it! Forget I even asked."

His mother grinned. "I'm sorry. What was your last question. Size? They're all pretty much the same size, I think. One baby foot's just like every other baby foot. It's not the same as adolescent feet." She glanced at J.P.'s enormous Reeboks.

"I still would love to know why you asked," she added.

"It's probably a math problem, Mom," Caroline said, looking up from the magazine again. "J.P.'s math teacher always gives interesting problems like that. 'If one knitter can knit one baby bootie in forty-three minutes, and one weaver can weave one tablecloth in forty-three days, then how long would it take the knitter to knit a tablecloth and the weaver to weave a baby bootie?' It's probably a math problem like that."

J.P. stared at his sister. "Caroline," he said, after a long moment, "you're an idiot. I hope you flunk fifth-grade math."

Caroline tossed her head and turned back to the article she was reading in *Newsweek*.

"I'm going to take a shower," Joanna Tate announced. She got up from the couch and started toward the hallway of the apartment.

"Wait!" J.P. said. He got up and followed her, bumping the corner of a table and stumbling over a footstool on the way. "Wait just one minute! I need you to do something for me. I need you to *knit* something for me, Mom."

Joanna Tate stood in the hallway and listened, nodding, while he explained earnestly.

"Sure," she said, laughing, when he had finished. "I can do that. You're a genius, J.P."

Eleven

"Lady, I ought to charge you a whole lot extra for this stuff. A *whole* lot extra," the cabdriver grumbled as he loaded the two golf bags into the trunk of the taxi.

"Come on," Joanna Tate told him impatiently, "it's no worse than a couple of suitcases. Pretend you're taking someone to the airport.

"Here, J.P.," she said, and handed him some money for the cab. "Don't give him too big a tip," she added in a whisper. "He's a grouch.

"Have fun," she called from the front steps as

Caroline and J.P. got into the taxi. "Happy Fling! Watch that antenna, Caroline!"

Caroline, wearing her bumblebee suit, ducked carefully into the cab, watching to be sure that the antennae didn't catch on the doorframe. J.P., dressed in his regular school clothes, climbed in beside her after watching the golf bags being safely stowed in the trunk.

The main brick building of the Burke-Thaxter School was festively hung with banners proclaiming spring in various colors. Bunches of helium-filled balloons, attached to each window, swayed in the light May breeze. Garlands of crepe paper flowers decorated the wrought-iron fence that bordered the building in front.

The sidewalk was crowded with teachers, parents, and kids, many of them in costumes. One mother was making final adjustments on a bright yellow daffodil hat that her first-grade daughter was wearing.

"Rats," Caroline muttered, looking through the cab window as they pulled up. "More bumblebees. I *knew* it!"

"There are always lots of bees, jerk," J.P. reminded her. "I told you you should think up some other costume."

"Look at Stacy!" Caroline pointed. "I wish we were rich. Her parents *bought* that costume."

J.P. looked. Stacy Baurichter, Caroline's best friend, was waiting on the front steps, swathed in lavender chiffon; attached to her back somehow were two gauzy butterfly wings. She waved, and Caroline, oddly pudgy in the striped bee body she had made by stuffing a leotard, ran over to join her on the steps. Her antennae wobbled as she took the steps two at a time.

J.P. paid the cabdriver and picked up the two golf bags that the man had deposited on the curb. He looked around for Angela, who had promised to meet him.

"Hi, J.P." It wasn't Angela. It was Hope, dressed in her everyday school uniform of skirt and pale blue blouse. "Angela's in the art room waiting for you. I told her I'd watch for you and let you know. Can I help carry something?"

"Thanks." J.P. gave Hope one of the golf bags and

followed her up the steps, making his way around the crowd of giggling kids. The day was to start with a parade of costumed students around the block. Very soon the teachers would begin to try to impose some order and get the kids lined up. J.P. could see the huge BURKE-THAXTER banner that two high school seniors would carry in the lead; at the moment they were leaning against the building talking, and the banner, folded on itself, read BKEHXER.

Nearby, some band members were taking instruments out of cases and playing a few warm-up bleeps on clarinets. Burke-Thaxter, which was a very small school, had a terrible band. Seven clarinets, one trumpet, four flutes, and a drum. That was it. A tenth-grade girl named Anna Vlados was such a good cello player that she sometimes performed with whole adult orchestras. But you couldn't drag a cello down the street with a marching band. So Anna Vlados — J.P. could see her talking to one of the flutists — was today wearing white tennis shorts and shirt and a reddish-blond wig; she had a sign on her back that said BORIS BECKER, and her cello was nowhere in sight.

Down the street, J.P. could see, residents of the brownstones in the quiet neighborhood were emerging from their homes and waiting on the sidewalk to watch, as they did every year.

He followed Hope to the art room, the two of them dragging and thumping the golf bags up the stairs. Angela was waiting there, leafing through a book of Picasso's paintings. She smiled a greeting. "Are you feeling all right today, James?" she asked.

"Yeah, I'm fine."

Hope looked puzzled. "Have you been sick, J.P.?" she asked.

"No." His voice was abrupt. "I'm fine."

Angela gave him a sympathetic, knowing, private look. "I asked Hopie to help," Angela explained, "because I suddenly realized that we need someone to stand us up, after we're inside our costumes."

J.P. blinked. He hadn't thought of that. "Good show, Angela," he told her, British fashion. "Let me go first, because I'm heavier and I may need two of you to stand me up."

He slithered into the green bag, and together

Hope and Angela took his arms, which extended from their armholes, and pulled him upright.

Next Angela wiggled into the red plaid bag. When she announced "Ready," Hope pulled her to her feet.

Walking awkwardly with tiny steps, their heads protruding from the tops of the golf bags, Angela and J.P. made their way down the stairs and out to the front of the school to take their place in the Spring Fling parade. Hope followed them, ready to prop them upright again if they lost their balance. It was very tricky, walking while wearing a golf bag.

Outside, Kevin Kerrigan called "Hey!" and J.P. looked over at the sound of his voice. Kevin was wearing a bathing suit, flippers, and snorkeling mask. He had plastic seaweed, with a rubber fish entangled in it, dangling around his bare shoulders.

"One o'clock, in the library!" Kevin called. He smirked arrogantly at J.P. "You ready? Ready to get beat?"

J.P. glared at Kevin, at the gaudy bathing suit, the pink rubber snorkeling mask pushed up on his forehead, and the hearing aid visible through Kevin's curly dark hair.

"Sorry, Kerrigan," J.P. called back. "I can't hear a word you're saying!"

Beside him, Angela waved to someone. To J.P. she explained, "That's my father. See him over there, wearing the striped shirt?"

J.P. followed with his eyes to the place she was indicating with her hand, and saw the distinguished-looking man who wore a striped shirt and horn-rimmed glasses. The man waved to Angela.

"I'm terribly eager for you to meet him," Angela whispered.

"Yeah." J.P.'s voice was noncommittal. The famous doctor was the last person in the world he wanted to meet.

"We'll find time later. Maybe after the chess match."

"Sure," J.P. told her.

"Let's get these lines sorted out, kids!" Mr. Goldfine, who looked absolutely ridiculous in his yellow and black bird outfit, was indicating where people should stand. Ahead, the Burke-Thaxter banner had been hoisted and was held aloft by the two seniors who would carry it down the street.

The seven clarinets tried to start a marching melody, faltered, and stopped. The drum thumped once. The clarinets began again.

"Look who he's with!" Angela said.

"What? Who? What are you talking about?" J.P. asked. He was trying to move into the position Mr. Goldfine had directed him to, but it was hard to move in the stiff, unyielding bag. He felt as if his feet looked like ballerina feet, tippy-toeing around with his ankles wedged together inside the golf bag. And he was *hot*. Sweat was trickling down his back, and the day had barely begun.

"My father," Angela said impatiently. "Look who he's with."

J.P. glanced over to where Dr. Galsworthy stood on the sidewalk talking to a middle-aged couple dressed in serious corporate clothes. Dark blue suits, both of them: man and woman. The dark blue wool suits looked only slightly more comfortable than golf bags.

"I don't know who they are," J.P. said irritably. "Get in line."

"Move out, guys!" Mr. Goldfine bellowed. The clarinets were at it now, full blast, and the one trumpet now and then. Those not in costume, including Hope, dropped back to the sidewalk. Only the costumed people were to march.

Sweating, J.P. hobbled along beside Angela. In front of them, some first-graders in duck outfits made from yellow rain slickers giggled and quacked as they marched.

"It's the Myersons, silly," Angela said. "They look exactly like the photograph of Raymond. Don't you even recognize your own aunt and uncle?"

The drummer at the head of the line thumped away with a regular beat. J.P. marched. His eyes swept the crowd on the sidewalk, jumping over Dr. Galsworthy and the Myersons with humiliation and a feeling of doom. Hopie waved happily from where she stood.

J.P. wished that his weird friend Ralph was there. Ralph, who understood about stupidity and adolescence and who was able to brush it all away with a wave of his hand in order to concentrate on real stuff.

"Quack, two, three, four." The ducklings giggled, marching importantly.

I, J, K, L. He said the letters to himself in order, in the same rhythm as the ducklings. That's what he and Ralph had gotten to. I, J, K, L.

Imbecile.

Jerk.

Knucklehead.

And loser.

Loser in chess. Loser in love. Loser in life.

TWELVE

J.P. STOOD HELPLESSLY, all alone.

Helplessly, ha. The word should be "hopelessly," J.P. thought, without any amusement at all, wishing that Hope were nearby to give him a hand. But not even Hope Delafield, who had proven to be such a help and such a friend, could help him now. He was in the boys' bathroom.

Here he was, standing upright in an idiotic stiff canvas golf bag. And he had to pee.

Through the door he could hear the noise as the student body and faculty and guests all trooped up the stairs toward the school chapel. Now that the parade was over, everyone was headed to the chapel for the opening ceremonies of the day.

No attendance would be taken at school today. Usually the teachers counted heads at chapel each morning, to make certain no one ducked out. But today, no one would notice if J.P. was missing or late.

Angela would notice, he realized. Angela would be sitting—no, she would be *standing*. Angela couldn't sit. Neither could he.

J.P. squirmed inside the golf bag. This costume was the dumbest thing he had ever thought up in his entire life.

He waited, standing in the middle of the deserted bathroom. Surely someone would come in soon, someone who could help him lift this golf bag off. Anyone at all—it wouldn't matter who. Mr. Goldfine, even, wearing that dumb bird suit. Even his archrival, Kevin Kerrigan, would do.

But through the door, the sounds of footsteps tapered off. Fewer people passed by. J.P. glanced at his watch and realized that the chapel service would be starting.

If he could just lie on the floor, he could wiggle his way out of the bag. But how on earth could he lie down when he couldn't bend his legs? He would have to fling himself onto the floor, which was covered with hard, white tile. One whomp with his head on that, and he might be a goner.

He squirmed again. He *really* had to pee.

But did he have to pee bad enough to risk a fractured skull?

J.P. eyed the floor, assessed his own discomfort, and decided that he could give it two more minutes. He would wait two more minutes for someone to come into the bathroom and save him. At the end of two minutes he would throw himself to the tile and probably die.

There was a knock at the door.

A knock? People didn't knock at a door that said GENTLEMEN on it in very plain black letters. They simply walked in.

But there was another knock.

"Yeah?" J.P. called.

"J.P.? Is that you?" It was Hope's voice.

"Yeah."

"Are you okay?"

J.P. hesitated. "Not exactly," he said, at last.

"I saw you go in there and then you never came out," Hope called softly. "So I got worried."

"Is there anyone out there in the hall?" J.P. called through the door.

"No. Everyone's at chapel."

"Well," J.P. called in a resigned voice, "there's no one in here but me. So you might as well come on in."

Ten minutes later, J.P. and Hope made their way up the stairs to chapel.

"Thanks, Hopie," J.P. whispered as they slipped inside as quietly as they could.

"No big deal," she replied.

His gratitude was very real. When he had explained his predicament, Hope had matter-of-factly helped him out of the golf bag, waited for him in the hall, and then helped him back in.

J.P. spotted Angela standing against the wall. He joined her there. They were the only two people in the chapel who weren't able to sit down. Angela looked a little angry.

"Where were you?" she whispered. "I was looking all over."

"Shhhhh."

"Are you all right?"

"*Shhhhh.*"

J.P. faced resolutely front, not looking at Angela. There was no way he was going to explain to her about the problem he had had. It was just too embarrassing. People like Angela wouldn't understand, anyway. People like Angela—*perfect* people—never had to pee.

On the stage at the front of the chapel, a group of third-grade girls dressed in bluebird outfits were singing, "Welcome, sweet springtime, we greet thee in song." When they had finished, they curtsied and everyone applauded.

The school's headmaster stood and made a series of announcements:

Refreshments available all day long in the courtyard behind the main building.

Balloons imprinted with the school logo for sale in the bookstore.

Gymnastics exhibition at eleven o'clock.

Dancing for all ages, with live music, seven clarinets, drum, trumpet, four flutes, and a cello, in the gym all afternoon. Come and go as you please.

Chess tournament finals in the library at one. Kevin Kerrigan versus J.P. Tate.

Kindergarten play about rabbits and elves starting right after chapel, in the basement kindergarten area. Everybody welcome.

J.P. watched the kindergarten children poke each other in excitement at the announcement of their play. He yawned. His knee itched, and he couldn't reach it. Beside him, Angela shifted her posture.

"This isn't terribly comfortable, is it?" she murmured.

He grunted something in agreement. Angela sure used the word "terribly" a lot. He hadn't realized that until this very minute.

Finally the headmaster put his list of announcements into his folder and looked out to the crowd seated in the chapel.

"One final and important thing before I dismiss you to enjoy the day's events," he said. "We have very special guests with us today." He looked down into the first row. "Would you stand, please, so they can see you?" he said to the couple seated there.

J.P. looked, and groaned silently. Mr. and Mrs. Myerson stood up and turned around so that all the students could see their Brillo hair and their boring faces and the fronts of their very boring blue suits.

"These are the parents of our student Raymond Myerson, whom some of you older folk will remember," the headmaster went on, beaming at the Myersons.

"Raymond was a fine boy, a fine student, a fine citizen," the headmaster said.

J.P. shifted from one foot to the other. His knee still itched. He felt sweat run down from his left armpit to his waist, where it caught in a puddle just above his belt.

The headmaster droned on about fine, fine Raymond Myerson.

"After Ray's tragic death—" He looked down,

suddenly, at the Myersons. "You don't mind if I call him Ray, do you?"

The Myersons flashed sad, proud, gleaming, very rich smiles. "Please do," Mr. Myerson said.

"After Ray's very tragic death in a boating accident at summer camp," the headmaster went on, "his parents decided to honor his memory with one of the most generous gifts ever made to the Burke-Thaxter School. Our science lab, the Myerson Lab, has been called one of the finest in all the independent schools in the United St—"

Rigid in her red plaid golf bag, Angela hitched herself slightly to the left, closer to J.P. "Did he say *boating accident?*" she asked in a loud whisper.

J.P. looked at the floor. "Shhhh," he said.

"And their gift today of Bausch and Lomb optical equipment, including twelve of the finest microscopes ever made"—the headmaster was going on and on, reading now from a paper of information in his hand. The Myersons continued to stand and beam.

"James, did he say *boating accident?*" Angela's voice was louder now.

"SHHHH!" Several people seated in the audience nearby turned toward the wall where J.P. and Angela stood side by side. Someone gestured, with a finger to his mouth, for Angela to shut up.

"Indeed," the headmaster droned on, "as a result of this impressive gift from the Myersons, we have decided to institute a new program at the high school level, a program in Marine Biology, which was, of course, our Ray's greatest interest, and the thing that he was pursuing at the time of the very tragic accident in which he died. A healthy, robust young man like Ray: such a loss. If he had not, it is fair to say, been reaching from the boat for a particularly interesting specimen, he might not, in fact—"

J.P. began to listen, with a grotesque sort of interest, to the account of Raymond Myerson falling out of a rowboat when he tried to collect some sort of floating oddity. He also watched Raymond's parents with curiosity, mystified by their beaming enthusiasm for the lengthy account of their son's demise, the apparent bliss with which they were recalling Raymond, his steel-rimmed glasses probably still intact, floating upside down in a murky New Hampshire lake.

If they have all that money, J.P. was wondering—enough money to buy a whole science lab and twelve Bausch and Lomb microscopes—why the heck didn't they buy their kid some swimming lessons?

Listening to the speech, watching the Myersons, and wondering about Raymond's failure, by age thirteen, to have learned even the simplest dog paddle, enabled J.P. to divert his attention away from Angela, who was now tugging on his arm.

"I find this terribly, *terribly* peculiar, James," Angela was saying very angrily.

He pulled his arm away.

THIRTEEN

THE DAY DRAGGED ON. Usually the day of Spring Fling seemed to fly past and end too soon, even for J.P., who had always been more of an onlooker than a participant.

But today, it dragged. It got hotter and hotter, and J.P. became moister and moister, as he perspired inside his golf bag.

Angela became less and less friendly, less and less charming, and less and less desirable. She said "terribly" more and more often.

She pulled him along by the hand to various

events. The gymnastics competition, where they stood on the sidelines and watched J.P.'s sister win an award for the parallel bars.

"She's terribly good at sports, isn't she?" Angela said to J.P.

"She's okay."

"You're terribly quiet. And you never answered me about your cousin, James. *Was* it a boating accident? And if so —"

"I don't want to talk about it right now, Angela," J.P. interrupted her.

Angela looked at him suspiciously. "When, then?" she asked.

"Later," J.P. promised, miserably.

"I'm quite certain my father would like to talk to you later, as well," Angela reminded him pointedly.

J.P. sighed, and looked at the floor.

"Now for refreshments. I'm terribly keen on some lemonade." And she grabbed his hand and yanked him away again.

Standing beside Angela in the courtyard, J.P. chewed on a hot dog and watched the kids and parents milling around, admiring each other's costumes.

"Don't you want a lemonade, James?" Angela asked. She was filling her second glass from the spigot at the big lemonade urn.

"No." Angela was really amazing. J.P. hadn't dared to have even one drink because he was afraid he would have to head to the bathroom again. Yet Angela was on her second — gulping it down — and she had not yet, not *once,* gone to the ladies' room.

J.P. looked around the courtyard for Hope. There she was, on the side, eating an ice cream cone and watching everyone, the way he and she had stood together and watched last year. He waved when he caught her eye. Hope grinned and waved back. Then she gestured toward her own wrist and called something.

"What?"

Hope called again, more loudly. She was pointing to her wristwatch. "One o'clock! In the library! Don't forget!"

J.P. shook his head. "I won't. I'll see you there."

As if he could forget the chess tournament. J.P. reached around the golf bag he was wearing, and felt its bulging pocket. Weird, having golf bag pockets to carry stuff in. But there it was, still safe, the special item he had brought, in the zippered pocket that would normally hold golf balls.

It was twenty minutes to one. J.P. glanced around again, looking for Kevin Kerrigan, but his enemy was not in the courtyard.

He's probably in the library already, J.P. thought. Getting ready. Plotting. Not plotting the Gruenwald Defense of a single queen's pawn opening—because he *knows* my middle game is better than his. He knows I can beat him at chess.

He's plotting how to clobber me a different way. And luckily I've been warned. I know that he's got his friends and their distractions lined up.

And, J.P. thought, patting his golf bag pocket again smugly, I have a counterweapon.

"Come on, Angela," he said, remembering that she was his official partner for the day, "we'd better get to the library. It's almost time for the chess tournament."

"You're terribly impatient, James," Angela said, coolly. "Let me finish my lemonade at least, please."

She sipped. It was, J.P. realized in astonishment, her third.

The library was crowded with spectators, and electric fans were turned on to move the warm air around.

The chess board was set up on the center table, and the official—Mr. Donovan, the school janitor, who was also adviser to the chess club and a former city champion himself—sat in a chair to the side.

Mr. Donovan was wearing a tightly coiled wire, like a huge Slinky, around his body. J.P., who hadn't seen him earlier in the day, looked at him in surprise.

Mr. Donovan rolled his eyes sheepishly. "I'm a spring," he explained. "It seemed like a great idea at the time."

J.P. laughed. "Well," he said, "at least you're flexible. You can *sit*. That's more than I can say." He hopped, in his golf bag, over to the table.

Kevin Kerrigan, in his bathing suit and flippers, was already sitting at the chess board. The official draw had decided that J.P. would be white, and therefore go first, in the first game. The tournament was best out of three, with a half-hour break between games.

One year the chess tournament had lasted into the night. But J.P. was pretty certain he could take Kevin quickly, in two games.

The spectators grew quiet, conversation halting, as J.P. approached the table.

"Just a minute, folks," Mr. Donovan said, in a loud voice. "I don't think anyone would mind if we allow Mr. Tate to take his very original costume off, so he can sit while he plays. Can I help you off with that golf bag, J.P.?"

Kevin stood up angrily. "No fair! I'm wearing *my* costume, so J.P. has to wear his!"

J.P. stood silently, waiting.

"But, Kevin," Mr. Donovan explained, "J.P. can't *sit* in his costume. He'll be uncomfortable!"

"So?" Kevin said. "You think I'm comfortable in this snorkeling gear? I have all this fake seaweed and stuff around my neck. So I'm just as uncomfortable as he is."

"Kevin—" Mr. Donovan began.

J.P. interrupted. "I'll leave the bag on, Mr. Donovan, and play standing up. Thank you anyway. But Kevin's right. He's wearing his costume, so I'll wear my costume.

"In fact," J.P. went on with a sigh, "I'll even wear my *complete* costume." He unzipped the pocket of the golf bag, took out a huge red knitted bootie, and pulled it on over his head. There were two slits, knitted exactly to J.P.'s specifications, for his eyes.

Kevin exploded. "What's *that?* Make him take that off!"

"It's part of my costume," J.P. explained. "It's the knitted thing that golfers put over their golf clubs to protect them. Isn't that right, Mr. Donovan?"

"I don't play golf," Mr. Donovan said. "Anybody here play golf?" He called to the crowd around the room.

Countless hands shot up. Almost everybody's parent played golf. Even Angela's father, J.P. noticed, peering through his eyeholes, had raised his hand. Even both of Raymond Myerson's parents played golf.

"Is it legitimate golf bag equipment?" Mr. Donovan asked the crowd.

"Yes!" the golfers called in unison.

"So let's start the match, then," Mr. Donovan announced. "J.P., you move first."

Standing, J.P. looked down through his head bootie to the chess board. Carefully he made his move, using his king's pawn.

P–K4

While J.P. watched through his eye slits, Kevin, frowning, reached up to his ear and turned off his hearing aid. It was a substantial part of Kevin's chess game — the total concentration that his deafness allowed. Although the crowd was very still, there were the inevitable distracting small noises that any large group makes: a cough, a sigh, a sneeze, a whisper.

Kevin could hear none of them. It was a huge advantage for him. He reached forward and made his move.

P–QB4

J.P. recognized the Sicilian Defense to a king's pawn opening. He smiled inside his bootie. The noises of the crowd were muffled by the wool, which helped.

In the crowd surrounding the table, Kevin's cohorts began the distracting maneuvers they had planned. But J.P. didn't notice. He couldn't see Antonio, fidgeting and moving, on his left. Or Kevin's brother, Ryan Kerrigan, who pulled out a huge white handkerchief and began to wipe his nose with a flourish, to his right.

Next Antonio stretched and yawned widely, his open mouth drawing the attention of most of the people in the room. But J.P. saw nothing through the eye slits except the chess board. Nothing at all. Concentrating only on the game, J.P. made his next move and began the slow, relentless battle that he was quite certain he would win.

FOURTEEN

THE FIRST GAME TOOK an hour, instead of the twenty or so minutes that J.P. had thought he would need to beat Kevin.

Hope had been correct when she warned J.P. that Kevin was getting better. That he was practicing a lot. That he was becoming more ruthless, more of a risk-taker.

And J.P., of course, had not practiced chess, read about chess, or thought about chess since the day, three weeks ago now, that Angela Patricia

Galsworthy had entered the seventh-grade math class and taken the unoccupied seat beside his.

The head bootie helped. Inside his hot red woolen fortress, J.P. was alone with his brain. Through the narrow eye slits he watched only the board, only the chess pieces, only Kevin's hands.

Across the board, Kevin, himself fortified inside the silence of his turned-off hearing aid, concentrated on the game as well.

The crowd watched silently. Kevin's cohorts had long since given up on their distracting maneuvers and had drifted away toward the gym, where the sound of music indicated that dancing had started.

"Check." J.P.'s voice was terse. Upright still in his golf bag, he had reached down and moved his king's bishop decisively.

Kevin stared at the board for a long minute, and then moved his black queen over to protect his king and take him out of check. He glanced apprehensively across the table to J.P.

J.P. took Kevin's queen with his bishop. The spectators were very still. Mr. Donovan adjusted his glasses and watched the board. It was clear that the game was coming to its climax.

Kevin reached out smugly and took J.P.'s bishop with a knight.

It was exactly what J.P. had hoped he would do. He moved his queen's bishop from the far side of the board where it had been lurking, almost forgotten.

"Check," J.P. said.

Kevin bit his lip. He held his hand above his own king, contemplating a move to the left. To the right. Back? Forward? There was no safe place for his king to go.

Finally Kevin laid his beleaguered king on his side. "I resign," he said in a low voice.

"Fifty-four minutes," Mr. Donovan announced, looking at the clock. "Good game, both of you."

The crowd clapped, and J.P. took off his knitted helmet and wiped the sweat from his forehead.

"Second game will begin promptly at—let's see—two-thirty," Mr. Donovan announced, after checking his watch.

Angela appeared at J.P.'s side, with yet one more

lemonade in her hand. "I went out to the refreshment stand because I got terribly hot," she told him. "And after a while, the game wasn't very interesting. It moves along so slowly."

J.P. didn't answer. He was still replaying the final moves in his head with a kind of satisfaction. He wiped the damp hair from his forehead again.

"Good game, J.P.," Kevin called from the library door.

"Thanks. I'll see you in a little while," J.P. called back. Kevin wasn't so bad, really, he decided. He was competitive, that's all.

Angela was watching Kevin as he headed off toward the courtyard entrance and the refreshment stand.

"Doesn't Kevin have nice broad shoulders?" she said. "I mean, for someone our age. Compared to most boys—well, like you, J.P., for example. Your shoulders are terribly narrow."

J.P. looked down at himself, still encased in the ridiculous golf bag. He *was* narrow.

"I imagine he's a terribly good swimmer," Angela went on, still watching Kevin in his psychedelic bathing suit with the slick, glistening kelp dangling around his neck.

"Unlike your cousin, Raymond Myerson," she added meaningfully, and turned to look hard and long at J.P.

Suddenly J.P. felt not only narrow-shouldered, but stupid. He felt, he thought suddenly, a complete, total, utter jerk. And a prisoner, as well. J.P. felt imprisoned in a stiff, suffocating golf bag; he felt imprisoned in a ridiculous romance with someone who never went to the bathroom in her entire life; and he felt imprisoned in a complicated network of lies.

He wanted, more than anything in the world, to escape. He wanted someone to tell him *how*.

At that moment, he realized that he knew who that someone might be.

"By the way, James," Angela said, "I am still very eager for you to meet my father. I think the three of us should discuss your illness. He's right over there."

J.P. looked across the library to where Angela's father was standing and chatting with a group of parents.

"Not now, Angela," he said, firmly. "I can't talk to your father now. I have to concentrate on chess. And also—"

He hesitated a minute. Funny, how not very long ago, he would not have dared to say such a thing to Angela Galsworthy. He would have blushed and trembled and stammered. But now it didn't seem to matter.

"I have to pee," he told her, and left the library.

J.P. found Hope in the hall, and nudged her into the supply room nearby. It was a small room filled with shelves of paper and books, and there was a sagging, decrepit couch along one wall. J.P. had always suspected that some of the teachers sneaked in here between classes to smoke. But today it was empty.

"Would you help me get this off?" he said, urgently.

"Sure." Hope tugged on the golf bag until J.P. was free. Gratefully he bent his legs and swung his arms, restoring the circulation. "Thanks," he said.

"Do you have to go to the bathroom?" Hope asked. "I can wait here and help you put it back on again."

But J.P. shook his head. "This is weird," he told Hope, "and I don't have time to explain. But I need to go and talk to someone before the next game." He looked at his watch. "I have twenty minutes.

"Listen, Hope, I know we're not allowed to leave the school grounds without permission. But I'm going to. I'm going to duck out and run over to see someone in the park."

"Who?" Hope asked curiously.

"I'll tell you later. No time now. Meet me back here, okay, in fifteen minutes, so you can help me get this stupid costume back on before the second game?"

Hope nodded. "Okay," she said.

She called after him as he fled. "I forgot to tell you, J.P.! You really played like a genius!"

He hadn't turned back to acknowledge Hope's comment, but he had heard it, and he thought about it as he sped through the park to the place where Ralph always sat. Some genius, he thought. I have a phenomenal memory and a high IQ and I can repair TVs and program computers and I play chess better than anyone else in the school.

But unless I can get myself out of this stupid situation, within the next couple of hours I am going to have to face a distinguished doctor of genetic research and pretend to him that I have symptoms of a disease that probably doesn't even exist, and I can't even remember its name anymore—

He ran down the path toward Ralph's bench, and despite his gloomy thoughts, J.P. was aware of how good it felt to have legs again. For hours now he'd been encased in stiff canvas. He hated the golf bag with a passion. He decided he would never play golf in his life. Not even *miniature* golf.

"Whoa!" Ralph called to him. "What's your hurry?"

In front of the bench, J.P. came to a stop with a skid of his sneakers. "Hi, Ralph. I only have a couple minutes. I have to get back to school. But I wanted to see you."

Ralph tilted the visor of his baseball cap. "So here I am. Take a good look."

"I didn't really mean I wanted to *see* you, Ralph; I meant I wanted to talk to you." J.P. was panting a little, breathless from his run.

"So talk. What's on your mind? More diseases?"

J.P. shook his head. "I guess I wanted to talk about, well, character flaws. That's what you called them. You seemed to know a lot about character flaws. Remember when I kept saying stuff like fraud, and fabrication, and you said those weren't diseases at all?"

"You're boring me," Ralph said brusquely. "Nap time." He pulled his cap back down to shade his eyes. He made a snoring noise.

"No, wait! Please, Ralph! I don't have anyone else to talk to about it!"

"So is that my fault?"

"No. No, it isn't, Ralph. It's mine. But I don't know what to do!"

Ralph coughed. "Kid," he said, "listen. You got problems. Worse than bursitis or gum disease. And I can tell that as we move along in the alphabet, you're going to want to say mendacity and misrepresentation and perjury and sham—"

"I don't know what 'mendacity' means, Ralph."

"Lies. It means lies. It *all* means lies."

"That's me, Ralph," J.P. told him desperately. "I'm a liar. I really am. It's my character flaw."

Ralph shrugged. "No sympathy here, pal."

J.P. stood awkwardly in front of the bench, his shoulders slumped. "I can't stand it another minute, Ralph. But I don't know how to get myself out of it," he confessed.

Ralph stared at him for a long time. He coughed and wheezed. "What was your A?" he asked at last. "Acne. That was it. And your B—"

"Body odor," J.P. reminded him. "And then I had common cold, dandruff, eyestrain, floaters, and goose bumps—"

"Yeah," Ralph said, recalling the list. "Bunch of crapola adolescent stuff. Most of it you're stuck with till it goes away of its own accord. Character flaws, though—they're different. They don't go away. They get worse."

"I *know* that," J.P. said dejectedly.

"Unless," Ralph began.

"Unless what? What can I do?"

Ralph shrugged. "Unless you decide to call it quits. Just put an end to it. Won't work with acne or the common cold. Won't work with this emphysema, which is gonna do me in soon. But you can call it quits with lying, J.P. I would, if I was you."

"Just like that? Just quit? You make it sound easy. But I'm all caught up in this complicated—"

Ralph gave a loud fake snore.

"I'll try," J.P. said dubiously.

"So try," Ralph replied. "No big deal." He yawned, and closed his eyes.

"But I love this girl," J.P. whispered miserably, under his breath. "I did it because I love this girl."

Ralph squinted up at him irritably. "That little blond bazooka you brought by here the other day? The one that gave you goose bumps? You're blaming her for your character flaws? Gimme a break, pal."

J.P. looked at his watch. "I gotta go," he said. "I have to break a speed record getting back or I'll be late for something important. I'll see you later, Ralph. Thanks."

He turned to leave, jogged a few steps, then turned back. "Ralph!" he called in a surprised voice.

Ralph looked up impatiently.

"What I just said? About the girl? That was a lie

too, Ralph, and I didn't even know it! I was lying to *myself,* even!" J.P. called. "I don't love her at all!"

Ralph sighed, and shook his head. "See you around, kid," he said, and coughed.

Entering the school, J.P. glanced at his watch and winced. Two thirty-seven. He was seven minutes late for the chess game, and they were probably all wondering where he was. They had probably sent a scout to the men's room to look for him by now.

"Geez, Hopie, I'm late!" he blurted anxiously as he dashed into the supply room. "I have to get that golf bag on faster than Superman in a telephone booth!"

But the room was empty. The golf bag was gone. And so was Hope.

FIFTEEN

J.P. OPENED THE SUPPLY room door quietly and peered out into the empty hall.

"Hope?" he called in an anxious whisper. But there was no answer. From one end of the hall he could hear the sounds of music and laughter. The gym was at that end, and the afternoon dance was at its height.

He tiptoed across the hall to the heavy wooden door with gold lettering that said LIBRARY. Stealthily he turned the thick brass knob, opened the door a couple of inches, and peered in through the narrow opening.

He could see the backs of numerous silent people. Beyond them, he saw the chess table, and Mr. Donovan, still wearing his Slinky-like spring. He saw Kevin Kerrigan hunched over the chess board, his snorkeling mask still pushed up above his forehead, his face intent with concentration.

J.P. pressed his face against the crack in the door and stared in astonishment. He saw *himself*, facing Kevin. He was standing as he had for the length of the entire first game, rigid in the golf bag, anonymous in his knitted red bootie.

He watched himself reach out one arm and move a pawn.

He knew that it was Hope's arm.

Panic-stricken, J.P. scurried back across the hall and into the supply room again. He sat down on the sagging couch and looked at his watch. Two forty-five. He put his face into his hands. There was absolutely nothing he could do but wait.

He didn't have to wait long. Ten minutes later, the door opened and Hope entered.

"I lost!" she wailed in a muffled voice. J.P. stood and pulled the thick red knitted helmet off her head.

"I lost, J.P.!" she wailed again, and began to cry.

"Hey, Hopie, don't!" J.P. said uncertainly. He had never tried to comfort a weeping person before. But he tried, awkwardly and unsuccessfully, to put his arm over Hope's shoulders. Hugging a person wearing a golf bag was a little like embracing a gas pump.

"Here," he told her. "Let me pull this off you."

He deposited the golf bag on the floor, and Hopie went to the couch and slumped there, weeping quietly.

"It got to be two-thirty," she explained, sniffling, "and you weren't here, but I was pretty sure you'd be back in a minute—"

"I *should* have been," J.P. said, angry at himself. "I'm *always* on time to stuff. But somehow I got held up over there, and when I got back—"

"Well, they started announcing on the intercom that the second chess game was supposed to start. And *then* Mr. Donovan announced that if either player didn't show up, the game would be forfeited, and so I suddenly thought that I could get into the golf bag, and they wouldn't know——"

She looked up at him and giggled a little. "It wasn't *easy,* getting that thing on all by myself."

J.P. laughed too and looked ruefully at the green canvas bag lying on the floor. "Then you just walked into the library as if you were me?"

Hope nodded. "Yeah. Although 'walk' isn't the right word. Hopped, sort of. Good thing our feet look alike." She looked down at her sneakers, which were very similar to his, though smaller.

"And our arms," J.P. pointed out. They were both wearing the Burke-Thaxter regulation blue school shirt.

"But I lost, J.P.," Hope added disconsolately. "I started out okay, but I got flustered. I was more nervous than I usually am. I don't know why."

J.P. laughed. "Because you were wearing a golf bag and a head bootie and pretending to be me?"

Hope grinned at him. She pushed her red hair back behind her ears and smoothed it with her hand. "Yeah, I guess that's why. But *darn* it, J.P. I wanted to win, for you."

"Hope, I'm *glad* you lost! If you'd won, it would have been a disaster! If you'd won, you would have been champion, and everybody would have started congratulating you, and you would have had to take the head thing off, and—"

Hope cringed. "And it wouldn't have been J.P. Tate at all."

"And it would have been cheating! But because you lost—well, heck, there's no reason for anybody ever to know. I'll just go back and play the last game. What time is it supposed to start?"

"Three-fifteen."

"That's in ten minutes. I wonder if I have time—"

"Time for what?"

"Hope, I'll meet you back here just before three-fifteen for the last game. I *promise* I'll show up. I just want to go find someone first."

She glared at him. "J.P., you're not going back to the park, are you? Because I'm *not* going to put that golf bag on again. I swear I'm not. There's a limit, J.P., to what I'll—"

"Honest. I'll be right back. I just need to tell someone something."

Leaving his costume behind in the supply room, J.P. dashed out into the hall and looked around. There. There at the end, near the gym entrance, Angela was standing with her father. Her golf bag had disappeared.

"Angela!" he called.

She looked at him casually as he approached. "I'm sorry I didn't go to the second chess game," she said. "But I got to talking to some friends out in the courtyard, and I completely forgot about it.

"I'd like you to meet my father, James," she said. "Father, this is James Tate. Those foolish costumes were his idea. I see you took yours off, too, James," she added. "I found it terribly difficult to dance, wearing a golf bag."

J.P. shook Dr. Galsworthy's hand politely.

"I lost the second game," he explained, though she hadn't asked. "The third one starts in about five minutes. So I have to rush back. But I just wanted to tell you something, Angela. I *don't* have that disease. I never did. I can't even remember what it was called; I made up the name, anyway."

Angela stared at him.

"Disease?" her father asked.

"Yessir. Angela told you I had this rare disease, and I know you were interested because you specialize in rare genetic diseases. But, sir, I just said it to make Angela feel sorry for me because I wanted her to like me."

The bell that signaled an announcement suddenly sounded, and everyone was quiet.

"The third and final game of the chess tournament is about to begin in the library." It was Mr. Donovan's voice.

"Rare genetic diseases?" Angela's father said. How about that, J.P. thought, suddenly; he has echolalia, too.

"I have to go," J.P. said in a rushed voice. "But I wanted to tell you I'm sorry. I'm sorry, Angela. I'm sorry, Dr. Galsworthy. I lied, and it was dumb and adolescent, and it was a character flaw.

"But I've quit lying," he said, and felt a great weight lift. "And I *really* have to go play chess now."

He turned and hurried back down the hall. Behind him, he heard something that he would think about later. He heard Angela's father say,

"Angela, what ever was that boy talking about? And why did you tell him that I'm a *doctor?*"

An hour later, J.P. ceremoniously dumped his golf bag into the trash can at the entrance to Central Park. Fourteen seconds after that, a jogger, breathing heavily, stopped, looked at it with interest, pulled it out of the can, and continued jogging with the golf bag in his arms.

"Wait till he finds out it has armholes and shoulder straps," J.P. said to Hope, who chuckled.

"Who is this guy you want me to meet?" Hope asked as she walked beside J.P. through the park.

"Just someone I know. He's a kind of philosopher. His name is Ralph."

He was afraid that Ralph wouldn't be there. He was afraid that Ralph would simply have disappeared, that he would remain forever a mysterious figure, so that in the night, for years to come, J.P. would stare at the ceiling wondering, "Did I dream it? Was Ralph only my own fantasy?" the way people did in books. And then, in the books, they would find some hint—some clue—some mysterious object, like maybe a piece of grubby cloth that could *possibly* have been a corner of Ralph's crummy handkerchief—they would find that lying around, to tantalize them, to make them always wonder . . .

But there he was, no fantasy at all. There was Ralph, blowing his nose loudly into his filthy handkerchief.

"Hi, Ralph!" J.P. said.

"You again."

"Yeah, me again. I did it, Ralph! I told the truth! And I won the chess tournament, and—oh, I almost forgot. This is Hope. Hope, this is my friend Ralph."

Ralph folded the handkerchief and replaced it in his pocket. He bent over, coughing for a minute, and then looked up.

"Hope," he said, appraising her with his inflamed, watery eyes. "Not a bad name. An H. H for Hope."

"And H for honesty, Ralph," J.P. told him. "How about that? We could do a whole alphabet of character—what's the opposite of flaws?"

"Attributes," Hope suggested.

"Yeah, character attributes! How about that,

Ralph? I already have the one that comes after honesty. *Integrity.*" J.P. glowed. He felt filled with honesty and integrity and all the attributes to come. "How about it, Ralph?"

Ralph peered at him skeptically. "You do what you want, kid," he said. "Whatever turns you on. Me, I'm gonna feed pigeons, okay?" He pulled a plastic bag of bread scraps from his pocket.

"Come on, J.P.," Hope said. "I want to go up to the pond and see if anybody's sailing model boats. Bye, Ralph! I'm glad to have met you!" She waved politely and ran on down the path.

J.P. watched her. Behind him, the pigeons made chuckling, murmuring sounds as they took the bread from Ralph's hands with nervous pecks. The sun caught Hope's hair as it bounced on her shoulders; and just for a minute—well, maybe only a second—it looked, J.P. thought, like *burnished copper.*

He began to laugh aloud. The image had lasted for only an instant. When he looked again, it was just his redheaded pal, Hopie. Behind him was not a mystic, not a philosopher, but just a wheezing guy named Ralph.

And himself? He was nobody but ordinary old J.P. Tate.

But he did feel, when he ran ahead to catch up with Hope, that for the first time in ages he was almost weightless, and completely unencumbered.

Just the Tates!

Read all the books about Caroline and J.P.!

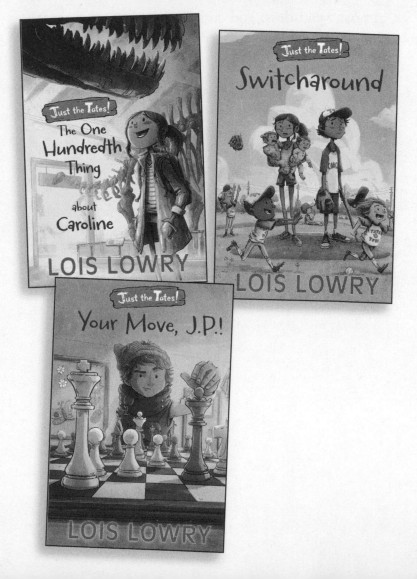

Just the Tates!
The One Hundredth Thing about Caroline
LOIS LOWRY

Just the Tates!
Switcharound
LOIS LOWRY

Just the Tates!
Your Move, J.P.!
LOIS LOWRY

There's no one quite like Anastasia!

Enjoy all her antics in the

Anastasia Krupnik series by Lois Lowry!